FROM SURREY

Edited by Lucy Jenkins

First published in Great Britain in 2000 by
YOUNG WRITERS
Remus House,
Coltsfoot Drive,
Woodston,
Peterborough, PE2 9JX
Telephone (01733) 890066

HB ISBN 0 75431 830 3
SB ISBN 0 75431 831 1

FOREWORD

This year, the Young Writers' Future Voices competition proudly presents a showcase of the best poetic talent from over 42,000 up-and-coming writers nationwide.

Successful in continuing our aim of promoting writing and creativity in children, our regional anthologies give a vivid insight into the thoughts, emotions and experiences of today's younger generation, displaying their inventive writing in its originality.

The thought, effort, imagination and hard work put into each poem impressed us all and again the task of editing proved challenging due to the quality of entries received, but was nevertheless enjoyable. We hope you are as pleased as we are with the final selection and that you continue to enjoy *Future Voices From Surrey* for many years to come.

CONTENTS

Daisy Tork 57
Katy Shenton 57
Alice Whitney 58
Marie-Claire Wyatt 59
Helen Crawford 60
Sarah Andrews 60
Heather Caddick 61
Michelle Chasey 62
Raeesa Chowdhury 63
Emma Halsall 64
Ashleigh Cheall 64
Alice Chilton 65
Harriet Ferguson 66
Sonia Goodman 66
Charlotte Mann 67
Emily Stanford 67
Amy Harmer 68
Charlotte Alexandra Souster 68
Melissa Rambridge 69
Mikaela Mills 70
Charlotte Haydon 70
Lucinda Lane 71
Helen Hudson 72
Lauren Parsons 72
Jocasta Jones 73
Amelia Lewis 74
Kate Marshall 75
Amanda Rea 76
Sarah Turner 77
Fiona Small 78
Pamela Jayne Stallard 78
Becky Watts 79
Charlotte Venables 80
Virginia Stacey 80
Elizabeth Stansfield 81
Stephanie Wells 82

Reigate School

Bobbi Hutchinson	82
Shelana Peerbeccus	83
Christopher Burr	84
Maxine Cronin	84
George Bateman	85
Simon West	86
Samantha May	86
Alistair Bance	87
Helen Kulka	88
Sam Wheeler	88
Laura Batten	89
Sarah Batchelor	90
Sam Causon	90
Alan Thomas	91
Helena Humpherson	92
Laura Nye	93
Lisa Glossop	94
Jennifer Briggs	95
Genevieve Noble	96
Emma Williams	96
Joe Costin	97
Samantha Tyrrell	98
Joanne Pedley	98
David Cadwallader	99
Kathryn Blake	99
Elise Reason	100
Daniel Allen	100
David Waring	101
Alan Robb	102
Louise Catt	102
Matthew Izard	103
Brett Avery	104
Morgan James	104
Charlotte Lucas	105
Lauren Best	105
Katie Smith	106
Joanne Dalley	106

The Poems

DO THEY KNOW

Do these men know they'll die?
Walking alone, their mothers cry.
Down the roads of uncertain death,
Not one of them speaks, not a single breath.

Do these men see the man-made hell.
That will cast over them in a blood-filled spell?
They'll fight for themselves and each other
Or most of all, for the tears of a brother.

Will these boys go home again?
Untrained boys amongst, fully trained men.
Scared of the sight up ahead
They're already there, they're already dead.

Heather Eggleton

PROFESSOR, PROFESSOR

Professor, professor worked so hard
in his back yard.
He had a dog on guard so
nobody could come into his yard.
Professor bought a new house,
he saw a little mouse!
Professor looked in the mirror to see
his face so he could tie his lace
and he could run with pace!

Asmah Haque (12)

NIGHT RAVEN

Fly doth the black raven,
Night's ancient dark beauty.
Whilst his wings still draw,
The night's dark star will live.
Raven's blood, crimson red,
A red so deep, so dark,
Drops like rain from above.
Bleeds doth the dark bird,
Weakens, stumbles, falls.
On cold ground he'll lie,
Finished, folded on the soil,
Never to fly in his black beauty.
As his sacred soul doth leave,
Wings stir in night's breath.
A spirit set free to fly the night,
This eternal star,
Will never bleed again.

Riehen Sutton (13)

SHELL SHOCK

In his eyes I looked, I saw such fear,
Fear like no other man's I'd seen before.
Here it comes I hear its roar,
Dead men scream 'I think it's war.'
Then he came at me like a beast from the dark,
His face coated with blood,
He fell at my feet,
Down into the mud.
The man next to me stared
His eyes still burning with fear.

We stood for a minute staring into each other's destiny,
The bombing's noise came closer and closer . . .
And 'Run!' was the command,
'Run, run!' I turned and ran just as ordered, until I was alone,
I think of them there crying out for help,
I look up, all around, there's no one there,
They can't be found.
There they lay to this day,
Their bodies shattered to the ground,
Their cries echoing in my head,
Crush me into a million tiny pieces when I hear them,
For it is guilt that I have found
I should have gone back,
I should have died,
I'm sorry
I go now to tell you all the pain I have suffered
For it is my time to face death,
When I should have faced it all that time ago.

Nicky Penton (13)
Commonweal Lodge School

THE CAT

The sleek, precise movements of the jungle cat,
As she glides along the jungle floor.
The black panther stirs and wakes,
The yawn turns into a menacing grin.
The beast rises; it turns and follows the wild rabbit.
She stalks her prey.
As she leaps in for the kill; she has no thoughts at all.
After she begins to regret that in the sudden moment of haste,
It took its prey.
The black panther with the gleaming black coat,
Stifles another yawn and sleeps.

Perdita Hall (13)
Dunottar School

WE'RE GOING TO HAVE AN UNHEALTHY TEA

We're going to have an unhealthy tea,
My sister, my mum and me.
We usually have something healthy,
Tomato, cucumber, Dairylea.

But tonight it's fried egg,
Chips and baked beans.
We'll wolf it all down
And split all our seams.

Here comes the cake,
'Oh for goodness sake'
Said my sister, mum and me.

Elizabeth Foreman (13)
Dunottar School

PEACE

Peace is a poppy field, full with the colours of your heart,
The same poppy field in which I can laugh, I can run and I can dart
And as I lay in the swaying grass and gaze up at the setting sun,
I ask myself, 'Is this peace and is it really fun?'

Peace is the draping willows that sway calmly in the breeze,
The conifers that fall over the world and fill it with auspicious ease.
The blossoms fall like soft lambs' fur that come from a mighty cloud
And Mother Nature whispers, 'This is peace, you should be proud.'

But then hurrying through the grass, trying to escape his evil death,
A young, weak soldier that dare not stop for a breath.
He is thinking, 'There should be none of this,'
As behind him a gun is fired,
The young soldier falls down at once, because now he is hurt and tired.

Peace is a graceful swan on top of a velvet blue lake,
Continuously swimming calmly as if not to let the water break.
It carefully lowers its long slender neck, that does not bear a crease
And as he does, yet being aware, he wonders, 'Is this peace?'

But who shall know and will we really care
When we find the answer that has always been there?
We can search and look and try to find the part,
The key, the answer, that leads to your heart.

Lydia Warren (13)
Dunottar School

HAVE YOU EVER CARED TO TAKE A THOUGHT?

The cold sinks through my clothes,
Prises through my skin,
To where my life's enclosed,
Here it slows my beating heart,
Freezing it to a marble plaque.

Love and hate are scarcely apart,
Life and death's woeful head come and leave,
Without usually ever being met.

Many say the world is ailed, many that it's void,
But I would like to set them straight,
The world alone is nothing,
Without the chaos of many minds.

Where would we be without pensive yet somewhat absent minds?
Many say without war,
With this I see their side,
But also have you cared to think where we would be
Without the solitude, chemist's cure?

The truth is: negative and positive are always interlinked,
A story never has less than two sides to its eternal being.

I will live and I will die, so will and do all you,
So listen to all the aspects before you find your life is through.

Although famine, disease, war and profound death
Will leave and breathe and never be totally quenched,
Try in everything you do,
You're not extinguished yet,
Live for your thoughts, your dreams and your mind's intent,
So that when you die something is still left,
The memory and pursuits that many will take with them.

Camilla G Tooley (13)
Dunottar School

ETERNAL SLEEP WITH ASH

My heart cracked like glass when I walked into the church
And saw her coffin.
I stared, I tried to hold back the tears
But I had been doing that for years.
She always made me cry.
Nobody knew her as well as I did, nobody cared as much as I did.
Life won't be the same without Ash.
Black everywhere, everyone was wearing black
So cold, so bleak, so boring.
Ash wouldn't have liked that.
Everyone was crying, why?
They never knew Ash.
As I walked up to her I seemed to be under an eerie spell,
As though someone had given me wings to approach her coffin.
What had made her so unhappy that she cut short her life?
When I found her she'd been so white.
I had lifted her hand, it was like holding ice.
Her lips had been icy blue,
She was in an eternal sleep.
Suddenly all the rage rushed out of me
Because of what she had done that night.
I was the only one that could understand her,
The only one that could communicate with her,
She could talk to me so why didn't she?
Why did she do it.
What was the cause?
I was stunned and amazed.
She looked at me with her wide blue eyes
That just stared right through me.
That was the memory of Ash.

Melinda Morrison (13)
Dunottar School

WHERE THE OLD MAN LAYS ALONE

Where the old man lays alone,
No one to love,
No one to care,
No one to laugh with,
No one to share.

Old and saggy were his clothes,
No wife to love,
No children to care,
No family to laugh with,
No friends to share.

He had no home,
Not even a shed,
Lived on dirty grey benches
Or slept on used newspapers,
Rotten and torn.

Miserable was the town,
Not caring for the homeless
And there he lays alone,
Without any money,
No food to eat,
No home to live in,
Not even a shed.

People passing by,
Laughing, talking, calling out jokes,
Wearing new fashionable clothes,
With family, friends and food to eat

And there . . . lays . . . the old man alone;
No one to love,
No one to care,
No one to laugh with,
No one to share.

Carishma Amin (14)
Dunottar School

EARTH

The continents of the world all fit in place
And this was the beginning of the human race.
It started with a bang
And then everything began
And the Earth started spinning round and round.

The world was once full of dinosaurs,
But that came to an end
And then things evolved
And the world began again.

The world now isn't perfect,
But it's quite a fantastic place.
There's poverty and violence,
However there is also style and grace.

Technology is advancing
And changing all the time.
Nothing stays the same,
In this wonderful world of mine.

The world will probably finish,
In a couple of million years.
So always be happy and fulfilled
And never cry a tear.

Joanna Sparber (13)
Dunottar School

FROZEN

Condensation runs down the window,
I peer out into the whiteness of the street,
Snow is falling, ice takes over my feet.
Each step is a crunch and a crisp,
Each breath is like a mist.
The silent sky is clear,
But the coldness is as cold as fear.
The frost has disappeared
And the snow, tired of rushing around in circles,
Drifted down,
Where it settled upon the ground.
The silence was shattered,
The song of a bird had begun.
The wind picked up,
The long, slender branches swayed
And then I made my way.

Elizabeth North (13)
Dunottar School

AN EARTHQUAKE

So still,
So silent,
Nothing moves,
The world has stopped or so it seems.

The clouds bob in their merry way,
The sky is blue on this glorious day,
The soft whisper of the wind swirls the trees
And beautifully spirals the tiny leaves.

The ground is shaking with excitement,
I hide away feeling very frightened,
Trees tremble, the sky clouds over,
Everything falls down closer and closer.

There's no way out,
I'm stuck,
Can't move,
So I slip away into a sleep of peace.

Kelly Fowler (13)
Dunottar School

SPACE

Space
An astonishing place,
A vast expanse,
A desolate uninhabited void.

Stars are sprinkled,
Like icing sugar on a cake,
Twinkling,
Illuminating the inky gloom.

These stars are distant,
Invisible to the naked eye,
But giant spheres of
Hot
Burning gas,
When viewed
From close proximity.

Laura Kerr (13)
Dunottar School

A STAR PERFORMANCE

The black sheet of night softly envelops the land,
A deep, velvet cloak wrapping sleep around creation.
The sun has set, the moon now rules
And her children, the stars, dance in the sky.

As we watch, the plough is pulled,
The celestial oxen in their silver harness
Grunt as they haul their eternal burden,
With the North Star at the head, the sailors' guide.

The Great Bear rears and bellows her call,
Shaking her vast, shaggy head.
Her companion, the Little Bear, leaps and plays,
Shedding specks of immortal light.

Still we gaze in rapture at the sky,
Watching Cancer and Scorpio battle it out.
The crab and the scorpion, both with their claws,
Fighting for dominance over the heavens.

Sirius, the Dog Star, chases his tail
And barks at the shooting stars
As Pegasus leaps up and over the moon,
His mane flowing like a streak of white flame.

The mythical creatures, framed in the stars,
Enchanting us with their fantastic games,
Slowly sink beneath the horizon,
Fading and disappearing one by one.

The moon vanishes as the dawn arrives,
Red and purple wash the sky.
We yawn and stretch - the new day is here
And the constellations sleep until night returns.

Helen Marks (13)
Dunottar School

THE FOX HUNT

The fox is getting away now,
The hunting dogs give chase.
The men are riding on horseback,
In an aggressive, vicious race.

It is not far to safety now,
To reach his humble home.
Just run a little faster fox,
There isn't far to go.

The dogs have caught the fox cub,
They go in for the kill.
The fox cub has stopped fighting,
He is lying so very still.

The dogs think the fox is dead,
But they are in for a nasty surprise,
For he leaps up and begins to limp,
Barely, but just about alive.

With their guns poised at the ready,
The men only shoot to kill.
To end the fox cub's pain,
To let him ache no more.

With nowhere else to go at all,
He bounds, skimming over a hedge.
But with the single piercing shot of a gun,
The fox is silent, lifeless, dead.

Jennifer Liddle (13)
Dunottar School

TO A SPECIAL FRIEND

Having a friend so true like you
So kind and caring,
So warm and loving
Who has helped me be me,
After so many times of trying to change,
To suit others who I thought were friends,
Has made me realise,
How lucky I am to know you
And I hope that to you
I'm the same as you are to me,
That you can talk to me
And trust me like I do you.
You never judge or criticise,
You know when I'm down
And help me get rid of my fears.
You never laugh at my worries,
But try to understand
And you always tell me the truth.
I know you respect me,
My feelings and my ways,
My doings and my beliefs,
My doubts and my habits
And all through my life,
As the years go by,
I will count myself lucky,
That I have a friend,
As special as you.

Lois King (13)
Dunottar School

FRIENDS

Whenever you are feeling down
Friends can make you laugh or frown
They're there for you when you need help.
Through troubled times you need not cry
'Cause friends are always standing by.

Friends can make you cry
Friends can make you laugh and smile
Friends can make you mad
They can also make you sad,
But whatever they do
They are always there for you.

Friends are the people who make you feel good
They don't bring you down
Or make you feel bad.
Friends are always loyal and kind
They tell the truth whatever is on their mind.

Friends are forever, friends are for life
And as time goes by
Their lives seem to change in many ways
It matters not how far or near
There will always be that special thing
That formed the bond between them.

Sometimes they stay together
Sometimes they don't
But memories will always be there
No matter what.
Some will be good, some will be sad,
Some will be happy, some will be bad.

Life without friends would be so empty
Never let the memories fade.

Louise Coates (13)
Dunottar School

FEELINGS

Tears sliding down a rosy cheek,
Heart torn to shreds.
Sickening pain in my chest.
Anger and hatred peer through my dark eyes.
Someone so close to my heart now gone.
Feeling used and beaten up inside,
Traumatised and ill with grief.
Why is life worth living?
Hours, days gone past in my life but no achievements made,
Sadness fills my eyes of darkness
And tears flood down like heavy flowing rivers.
Strong emotions for this person cause these sharp pains.
Oh why am I so badly hurt,
When I myself caused the pain between us?
Complicated matters do not mix with young minds
And should be taught to be resolved
But love seen in young eyes is a fantasy
Or tale that is yet to be read
Love should be lead by hearts not eyes.

Ashlie Harris (13)
Dunottar School

THE SEASONS

The cool and crisp chill,
That is in the fresh breeze,
Those bright colours all around,
The daffodils and newborn lambs.

That special summer sand,
The waves lapping at your feet,
The heat makes you tired
And you hope it will never end.

The classic cheerful sea of colours,
The leaves falling from high above,
That really refreshing breeze,
Now, what is going to come?

That shimmering sheet of snow,
Lying on the terrain beyond,
That stillness in the air,
Bringing everything to a cease.

Danielle L Bessant (13)
Dunottar School

CLOUDS

Clouds are like white puffs of cotton wool
They change direction
Some are thick and big
Some are thin and spooky
Some shield mystery
Who knows what is happening behind them?
Clouds are spontaneous with wispy-like hair surrounding them.
The sky is far away but clouds are quite near us
But it looks as if clouds are printed randomly on the sky.
When you are in an aeroplane,
Clouds are way below
But when we are on Earth,
They are way above us.
Clouds are pure white on a bright day
Pure grey on a rainy day.
The clouds seem to be dictating the weather.
Such control of our little white clouds.

Charlotte Barber (13)
Dunottar School

THE SHIP OF DREAMS

As she coasted through the darkness,
Who could tell what was to befall,
The huge luxurious liner with 2,200 people on board.

There was no moon that fatal night,
To give the water vital light,
Only lamps creating a pool,
Of shadows on the water cool.

So many ice warnings came through,
There was so much that they could do,
To prevent disaster, to save many lives,
But only 705 would survive.

Then all of a sudden out of the gloom,
A large lump of ice began to loom.
The watchmen rang the bell times three
And told Mr Murdoch what they could see.

Too late to turn,
But they still cried 'Full astern'
The iceberg hit and split her side,
Nobody knew that by the end of the night 1,500 would have died.

At first none believed that the great ship would sink,
But as the hull sank lower
It pushed human sanity to the brink.

As the stern finally went under,
Screams and cries rang out,
But were silenced by the cold of the water

And the people in boats,
Were forced to believe they were merely the cries of the damned.

Lisa K Gallo (13)
Dunottar School

BURNT

Burnt through the skin,
It tingles like the strangest of sensations,
The heat seeps through her,
Diffusing into her blood.

The pain tears through her,
Up her hand, her arm,
To her head
Invading like a troop of soldiers, preparing for war.

The agony is inescapable,
It leaves a severed path
Tearing at her veins with vicious spikes
Destroying all her senses.

The army set up camp.
All she thinks of now is the pain,
The inescapable, permanent scar of heat
Ripping at her nerves.

She tries to divert her thoughts
But she comes back to the pain.
Her mind never forgets that pain,
Leaving her senseless and numb,
Engulfed in the flames.

Nasreen Ahmed (16)
Dunottar School

LIFE

Towards the precipice, concealed by mist,
The horse stumbles, wheezing,
Caught in the reins she had dropped long ago.
Another boulder;
The wheel scrapes past, spokes catching; carriage shudders.
Another rut, the horse dimly reflected in the puddle,
Her gaze adjusts to see mud flecks on the window.

She can't see ahead; the front window is steamed up.
Her head hits the frame as she presses her face to the cold glass,
Sees the mist lowering ahead.
She's unable to see where the best route for their journey lies.
She clambers to the front, coaxing the mare to slow down,
It goes too fast for her to jump,
Too slow to pass the cloud
Which prevents her seeing the distant precipice ahead
Or indeed the close ground.
She tries in vain, grasses scratch her legs leaving lasting red blemishes.
The creature's force demands her resigned compliance; no use.

Fog behind has enveloped the winding track, except where the
Sunlight spotlights the rolled grass: noticeable as it's surrounded
By long, tawny arms swaying to a rock ballad.
To an observer it looks like a toy steam engine
Having run off the rails, destined for the unknown.
But there are no observers.
The one there might be shows no presence;
For there are no footprints beside the hoof hollows and the wheel ruts.
At least, not that she can see.

Nor does she see the other carriages, the millions
That criss-cross the grassland towards their own precipice,
Unseeable until it is upon them.
She doesn't see. They don't see her. They travel,
All on their own,
Looking out, slowing the horse in vain, wary of the mist.

Sarah Pringle (16)
Dunottar School

WHAT WE MAY BE

When all your plans go wrong
And your life just stops right still,
All your dreams have shattered,
Your friends have turned their backs
And you find yourself wondering how it will all end,

Turn and look in the mirror
And see the outer body of your soul,
This is what you should live for,
The tomorrow full of all the world,
Waiting for you and all you have to offer.

You always have to pick yourself up,
Not let yourself wallow in all your sorrow,
It will be lonely and it will be tough,
But if you can make it all alone,
You will be worth more than any other.

Every person has felt the lows and seen the highs,
Some have lost and some have won,
But it's always the end result of a person that matters
Not the circumstances that people sometimes endeavour.

Elizabeth Kitching (16)
Dunottar School

THE FLYCATCHER

The flycatcher snaps,
Snaps all day and night.

And if you are a fly,
It will give you such a fright.

As you'll find it is camouflaged
Between the leaves and trees.

Sometimes you'll cry for mercy,
Please don't call me, please.

And like all other plants,
It needs the sun and rain.

To change the CO_2
So we can breathe again.

Flies also need to breathe
And stop for a rest.

The plant cries out *'Yum, yum'*
And rids us of a pest.

And when the sun has gone,
The moon comes out to play.

Flies stopping for a rest
Won't see another day.

It only eats up flies
Not strawberries or bananas.

And as the moon comes up
It puts on its pyjamas.

Flies passing, don't be fooled,
This plant is quite unique.

You're in for a surprise:
Flycatchers never sleep.

Clare Cooper (11)
Dunottar School

GROWING OLD

One thing that scares me most in life is growing old.
I don't know why I feel this emotion.
It may be the scenes I have seen of elderly people in distress,
Watching them trying to cross the road at a snail's pace.
Their backs all hunched up leaning over their walking sticks,
Their hands curled around the handles as if they were stuck like glue.

My whole life is flashing before my eyes like a flash of lightning.
Growing old is an image I see in the near to distant future.
It felt like yesterday I was a little girl, running around the playground
At my old primary school,
Fighting over the clothes in the dressing up box.
I feel as if tomorrow will be the rest of my life.
The fear of gaining my own independence,
Meeting new people of different cultures, different lands.
Travelling to far away places the other side of the world,
Without the comforting sights of my friends and home comforts.

I wish I could remain young for my whole life,
Just like Peter Pan who was determined never to grow up.
I do not wish to live forever, just remain the age I am at the moment,
Would make me quite content,
For this would be a dream come true.

Francesca Tomkins (15)
Dunottar School

LIFE

What is life about?
So many ask this question.
So much to learn but,
So little time
How am I ever to succeed?

Life is so full of temptation,
I am expected not to stray,
But how can I not?
It seems much more fun that way.

But I know it is for my own good
To stay good and true,
To do what is expected of me,
The grades and all.
But what fun it would be,
To just have a taste
Of a different life,
One full of mystery and wonder,
What I would give.

But if I was to stray
What would happen to me?
That is what frightens me
For I do not want to waste my life
For it is precious to me
Although sometimes it is
So tedious, to be good

But I might as well struggle on
I know it is for the good
And maybe one day
I will look back and be glad that I did,
I hope!

Rea Jordan (15)
Dunottar School

AUTUMN

Awakening to the cold, dark mornings,
Condensation lying on the windowpanes,
I dare not venture out of the warmth of my cosy bed
To the freezing surroundings.
However with a burst of enthusiastic energy
I leap out from the warmth
And into my hot clothes which hang upon the radiator.
Breakfast now has changed from cold fruit
To a piping hot, filling porridge,
Which warms my body, ready to start a stressful day.

The lessons start bright and early.
However I find my mind elsewhere.
I gaze outwards to see the green trees turning golden,
Girls and boys running around with woolly hats and scarves.
As they trudge by, I hear the crunch and crackle
Of the crisp autumn leaves.

Yet the evenings are growing closer, shorter
On the way home to the warmth of my home,
I watch everyone in their houses huddled around the fire.
The evening meal suddenly changes from a light snack
To a heavy, hot meal.
The nights seem shorter with the long darker evenings
Causing my family to venture towards their bedrooms
Earlier than usual.
In the warmth of our beds we rest till the morning,
Awaking to the robin's merry song,
Ready to start a new day.

Ruth Hyde (15)
Dunottar School

THE FUTURE

When we are young, it is funny how we want to be old
And when we are old we want to be young.
We always want what we cannot have,
Only the future can tell where we will end up in thirty years' time.

At a young age you have ambitions and dreams,
Some may have their whole lives mapped out.
They are going to go to university and get a degree,
Not as easy as they think,
They say it as if it is a stroll in the park.
Only when they get to university will they work this out
For themselves.

Many people have a dream,
A dream of a family,
Two girls and a boy all planned.
They might even have chosen names.
Others may have a very different view;
'I am never getting married,'
'I hate children,' they will say.
Who knows, attitudes change through the course of life!

We all see the future as technology,
Robots doing everything for us
And everybody wearing silver clothing.
In 1990 everybody thought that this would be the picture
By the year 2000.
It is now 1999 and only a few months way from the year 2000,
I cannot see many robots,
Can you?

Cheryl Furness (15)
Dunottar School

I CAN TIE MY OWN SHOES

Where is my life heading?
How can I compete with them?
They know where they are going,
How will I get there and when?

The sun is setting on my childhood,
I am grown and can tie my shoes on my own,
Who is this crowd around me?
How come I find myself standing alone?

Swallowed in this faceless crowd,
Will anyone help, guide me through?
No, I am not young any more,
I know I can tie my own shoes.

Like a fairy tale will he rescue me,
My knight in shining armour?
Will I grow old and marry him?
Will he become a father?

What career will I have? I wonder,
Will I be a successful business girl,
Or shall I become a housewife,
Cook and clean and own my own pair of pearls?

Will my life take a tumble?
Will I become poor on the street?
No, I have to be strong,
I can walk on my own two feet.

I have to decide this moment
What am I going to do.
No one can help me get through this,
But I know I can tie my own shoes.

Victoria Ford (14)
Dunottar School

THE CHRISTMAS TREE

It is Christmastime, the tree is up.
It's been decorated from top to toe in baubles
tinsel and there is a fairy on top.
The lights have been carefully put on the tree . . .
crash there goes another bauble.

Three hours later, the whole family is standing round
the tree.
Waiting for the tree to glow bright red,
as the lights are turned on.
One, two, three . . .
it is still pitch black.

Hours later after checking that all the bulbs are
working correctly and climbing all over the tree,
there go another two baubles.
The family stands waiting for the glow of red light
to fill the room, one, two and three . . .

At last the room is filled with light.
The red lights of the tree send out warmth and
security.

For the rest of the evening, you start putting all the
Christmas presents under the tree and trying to guess
what they could possibly be.
You shake and feel them, to make sure it is not a pair of socks
or a woolly jumper from your great aunt.
This present you put to the back of the tree.
It is Christmastime.

Lauren Farley (15)
Dunottar School

THE TIGER

The tiger's body is a beautiful thing,
With beautiful black and orange stripes on its body.
The tiger is like a steam train as it ploughs through the
hot desert fields.
It moves swiftly in the grass and then it stops,
crouching down in the long desert grass watching its prey.
Waiting to make its move, there is a strange eerie silence.
The antelope knows that something is wrong.
As the antelope tries to run and be free of the tiger, he is too late
As the tiger makes an enormous leap and brings the antelope
Down! Down! Down!
Onto the dusty floor
and with one foul swoop it kills the antelope, bringing it to the floor
like a cold stone being dropped to the ground.
The herd of antelope see what has happened.
They start to run, run away from the tiger!
The poor tiger out of breath and tired from his previous kill,
lets the herd go.
The tiger can hardly move from the intense heat of the sun.
It slowly makes its way to the waterhole,
the tiger laps up the water like a sick dog.
The tiger slowly gets cooler and starts to get some energy back.
As the sun starts to set, the tiger ambles slowly towards a lonely,
deserted tree, which is shaded by the leaves and branches.
The tired tiger starts to climb onto a low branch,
where it can get some rest.
The tiger slowly falls into a deep sleep,
as tomorrow will be a new dawn, a new day and another life to kill!

Philippa Day (15)
Dunottar School

A Rose

Their thorns as sharp as needles,
Their touch so very harsh,
Their ever growing stems entwining
Within the walls of their grasp.

Rich red in their colour,
Like that of red blood;
A broken hearted maiden,
A look of sorrow on her face,
Her heart is so heavily laden
With the burden of true love

And yet their aura so beautiful,
So enticing, to captivate hearts and minds,
A reminder of love:
Presented from one soul to another,
A symbol of loving times.

A rose.

Charlotte Davis (15)
Dunottar School

Sunset

Growing slowly, ever bigger,
The orange sun sits in the sky,
Casts its glow upon the landscape
Lifts the heart and draws the eye.

Sitting high upon the hill
Watching as the colour changes
From gold to pink and purple sky,
Casts its shadow over you and I.

Gone is brightness, a fading sunset
A disappearing ball of fire.
All its glory soon forgotten
Sailing through a silken sky.

Goodnight sunset, slowly sinking
Taking all its bright white light.
Oh! What pleasure that you bring us
As you disappear from sight.

Michelle Howell (11)
Dunottar School

FRIENDSHIP

A firm and solid foundation,
I know she'll always be there.
Like a shadow always behind me,
Forever showing her care.

We always know we have each other,
Nothing can tear us apart.
She's part of my soul, deep within me
She will always remain in my heart.

A candle that burns for eternity,
Like a bright, strong yellow flame.
It flickers on the darkest days
But she's not always to blame.

A shadow changes with the weather,
Gets shorter with the sun.
But do I think she'll ever change?
The chances are a million to one.

Reena Patel & Katy Hallmark (14)
Dunottar School

DAYDREAMER

I dream of all the days,
When I'll be noticed for real.
For who I really am
And what's inside of me.

I don't come from a perfect world,
No matter how anyone can see.
There is darkness in my heart
And no light inside of me.

There's no one I can depend on,
No one there to care,
There's no one I can trust honestly,
My soul is grim and bare.

No one can see the truth
Beyond my perfect world.
The so-called 'golden life'
I don't want to play a part of.

I will escape the battle,
My emotions will not hide,
They'll take me to the front line,
Where every soul has died.

I think that soon I'll move,
On to better and brighter stars.
I'll escape this tangled web
And the rules I won't obey.

The future has a lot to offer,
But maybe not for me,
I hope the darkness will fade
And the light will shine through me.

Clare Griffiths (15)
Dunottar School

WINTER

It's cold outside,
All the trees are bare and swaying in the breeze.
The sky is grey and you can see the faint sun
Peeping out from behind the clouds.
The pond has frozen over and there are icicles
Hanging from the bird table.
You can hear the deep snow crunching beneath your feet
And leaving a track of footsteps.
The snowman made the day before just standing
Still doing nothing but watching the odd robin fly past.
All the animals have finished collecting their winter's store
And have hibernated into their warm beds like a baby in its crib.
Stockings have been filled
And the Christmas tree is surrounded with presents.
The Christmas decorations are all up
And everyone is indoors having fun.
Presents are being opened and children's faces lighting up
Christmas dinner being served and carols being sung.
The day gets older and is getting dark,
Crumpets are being toasted on the log fire
And sherry is being drunk.
Children playing with their new toys and eating their sweets
But soon are to get ready for bed.
The fire is put out and teeth are cleaned,
The hot water bottles are being made for the cold night ahead.
Everyone gets into their pyjamas
And then snuggles up into their nice warm bed,
Children are tucked in and kissed goodnight.
The lights turn out.

Lily Preece (14)
Dunottar School

THE BIN MAN

When autumn comes
And the leaves have fallen,
The Bin Man comes too.

A little old man,
Who all the children fear,
As he shuffles along the street,
Dragging a bin behind him.

He sweeps up the leaves
And shovels them into his bin,
No sound he makes,
Except for the swish of his broom.

As you pass him cautiously in the street,
He peers down at you with his beady eyes,
Past his long crooked nose,
On his slender weathered face.

This is all you can see of the Bin Man,
As the rest of his body is concealed,
By a long black raincoat
And a scarf that comes up to his chin.

When autumn passes and winter comes,
The Bin Man shovels grit to stop us slipping.
As the snow begins to settle,
Snowball fights begin.

'Accidents' they claim the children who throw snow at him
And he only reacts with a groan,
This is their warning to back off.

Although scary he seems,
One day I was proved wrong,
As I cycled by on the slippery path,
I skidded right into the road.

If it had not been for his rough hands,
That scooped me out of the road,
I would not be here today.

Now as I pass I greet him with a grateful smile,
From him I receive a warm smile too
And on the coldest of days I offer a hot drink,
Or for him to come in for tea.

Madeleine Gormley (14)
Dunottar School

THE SKY THROUGH THE DAY AND NIGHT

The sky in a night of winter
Is as deep as a deep black pit
The sparkling stars that shimmer and shine
Like candles just been lit.

The sky in a day of spring
Is as blue as pale blue can be
The clouds in the sky
Like white puffs of smoke
Are vague and hazy to see.

The sky in a night of summer
Is red and warm and kind
Whilst daffodils rest their gentle heads
Making their faces hard to find.

The sky in a day of autumn
Can be black, blue or red
And when this time of the year has gone
Everything seems still . . . dead.

Antonia Redgrove (14)
Dunottar School

NO ONE UNDERSTANDS ME
(BUT SOMEBODY MUST)

No one understands me.
I look in the mirror and cry.
I could never tell anyone my problems.
You feel like shouting your feelings out to the world.
You tell someone and they tell everyone.
You just want to be alone.
They don't understand.

You go for a walk with tears streaming down your face
They drop on the floor with a splash.
You feel like being buried alive because life is so bad.
You don't eat.
You don't sleep.
You forget about doing your work
But life slowly gets better
And it will go forward from now on!

Your friends, your family here to support.
You don't want their support, you want him back.
Every time you close your eyes you see his face.
He has such grace.
You feel you'll never forget about him
But as you finally mature,
The feeling goes.

Beth Hayman (14)
Dunottar School

MISTREATED

Eyes, like eagles watching over,
What people do,
She looks at me
Makes me feel unwelcome,
This dog, down the road

Looks and stares at strangers,
Policemen, milkmen and even residents,
Makes me feel tense, frightened
This dog, down the road,

Her fur looks soft,
But dirty, very dirty.
Her nails,
So long,
Eyes sad,
Neglected,
I look at her in a different light,
This dog, down the road,

I learnt her name,
Dog,
Not even a name,
So I named her Hope,
I am now good friends with,
This dog, down the road.

Sarah Travis (12)
Dunottar School

A TRAIN'S DAY

Here comes the train from the station below,
chuckaty chuck, chuckaty chuck,
come on people come run and go, *dideledi dum, dideldi dum,*

The train's on time and ready for fun,
tootaty toot, tootaty toot.
We pass houses and trees and farmer with dogs,
cattle and sheep and hundreds of logs.

Into the town we're still on our way,
shops and streets and children that play.
Buyers and sellers every other way,
people always say 'Hey!'

Out of the town onto the road, traffic jams and a heavy load.
At last we're here, 'Hooray! Oh yay.'
Out of the train and ready to say,
'What a lovely day it was today,
but I think I'll go the other way.'

Alexandra Inglis (11)
Dunottar School

AUTUMN

Summer's gone and autumn's here
It's a favourite time of year.
Leaves have fallen off the trees
Swept away by a chilling breeze.

Summer's flowers are almost dead
But holly's here with berries red.
Soon Jack Frost will come by night
Dusting the Earth powdery white.

Fallen leaves are everywhere
Leaving claw-like branches brown and bare.
When autumn's burning colours go
Cold winter covers them in ice and snow.

Sarah-Louise Jordan (11)
Dunottar School

GANGSTERS TRIPPIN'

Through the dark streets at the back of the estate.
Down the dark winding alleyways.
Around the derelict houses that are inhabited by pigeons and tramps.
Beyond the battered boxes by the wasteland meet the hardest gang
you ever saw.
There's Jimmy the leader and Blackeye and Stan.
With Dan and Thicko they wander round waiting for their opponents
to show.
Then through the bushes they come, two little year sevens they had
picked on at lunch.
They look like neon lights in the bleak landscape.
Or bright lights deep in space.
Slowly they approach the group.
Slowly but surely like a tiger waiting to pounce the gang stand up.
Then suddenly out of the silence, *bang, wallop, crash, ouch!*
Suddenly the gang stop, blue lights are approaching.
They leave the two boys and run into the distance.
But it's too late, they're surrounded.
All five of them get rounded up into a police van.
Paramedics surround the boys and soon they're off.
Soon the derelict wasteland is silent again.

Clare Gordge (14)
Dunottar School

PERFORMING

I walk onto the glittering stage,
And onto the judgement block,
I look up,
A sea of people,
All looking at me, tiny me.
Eyes, set like glass,
All expecting, waiting, judging
I begin to move,
Slowly, steadily.
A ruffle, cough, sneeze,
All produce one more bead of sweat.

My dance is over,
I slowly, warily stand up.
I hear one clap, two, three, four, five, six!
They are all clapping!
The butterflies had gone,
They had all flown away . . .
But I have to do it again tomorrow.

Claire Groves (12)
Dunottar School

DUCKS

It's fine for you
Smiling down at me,
Would you like
Wobbly legs and
Great big feet?

It's fine for you
Safe in your house,
Would you like
The worry and stress
A fox behind each bush?

It's fine for you
Warm in your bed,
But think for one moment
Of me in the straw
Shivering with fright.

Caragh Johnson (12)
Dunottar School

A WINTER'S NIGHT

As the lonely pale moon
glows in the midnight sky
which is as black as coal,
it shimmers a light.
Everything is still and quiet,
only the bitter cold wind
blowing on a winter's night
through the trees like a ghost.

The trees are dark with glaring faces,
that stare at you with beckoning calls,
and in their dark menacing shadows
something is lurking.

As the mist rises it sets an eerie feel,
the frost is forming which glistens
softly like glitter.
The ground is hard all around.

As the sleepy moon slowly fades away
and the dawn begins to break,
the feel of midnight has gone
and we are ready for a new day.

Charlotte Bendig (12)
Dunottar School

THE SPIRIT OF THE MERRY-GO-ROUND

Around and around it goes
Not stopping for anyone.
The spirit just turns and turns.

The eerie creak as the horses
Rise and drop at that steady velocity
The spirit just turns and turns.

No one dares go near as they are
Scared of its dizzy mind.
The spirit just turns and turns.

That's when the work begins
The uproar of the machinery.
The spirit just turns and turns.

That's when the shiny modern one comes
No more screeching up and down and
The spirit doesn't turn anymore.

The children are happy riding on the
Brand new space rockets zooming around.
The spirit doesn't turn anymore.

Now at the scrap heap the spirit lurks
Turning around causing commotion.
The spirit turns again.

Jessica Standen (12)
Dunottar School

MY NIGHTMARE LAND

Thunder *crashing,*
Booming rain,
I am having an awful nightmare again.
No colours around me,
Nobody near
This is the land of my worst fear
No sun no stars no light at all
People here treat you cruel.
Love and laughter is not heard here
Surely because the devil is near
Lightning strikes one two three!
No more people except for me
Now I do not know what to do
So I will pass this nightmare over to you.

Sabrina Bell (11)
Dunottar School

STRANGE GIRL

We went into the bushes where we're really not allowed,
But I knew we had to somehow get away from all the crowd.
I stroked her long blonde hair - it was matted up with twigs,
I kicked away some messy stuff that once had been some figs.
I sat down on a log, and she had me close my eyes,
I wondered what was happening - just what was the surprise?
I felt for my footing, and she held my hand,
The ground was soft - like muddy sand.
Her soft hands touched me and I flew through the air,
I landed in a ditch with a wisp of her hair.

Alex Bailey (11)
Dunottar School

CHOCOLATE

Chocolate, the name says it all.
No one can resist it,
especially not me.
I like chocolate for breakfast,
Coco Pops are the best.
Chocolate spread sandwiches
they're for lunch.
For tea, well, unfortunately they haven't got
chocolate for that.
For pudding though, it's ice-cream and lots of chocolate sauce.
Chocolate, well, without it my life won't be complete.

Nicolette Fowler (11)
Dunottar School

GRANNY

Some grannies are old and strict.
Some grannies are thin,
And some are thick.

Some grannies take you to the park,
Some grannies have little yappy dogs;
Some grannies have a big dog with a big bark!

But my granny lets me do anything;
Takes me to the cinema with my friends,
Get some popcorn or something;

My gran's totally round the bend!

Josephine Gordon-Wright (11)
Dunottar School

I'M BORED

I sit at my window,
I watch the rain,
I can't go out to play again.

The birds are hiding in the trees,
Do stop raining
Please oh please.

There is no one home to play a game,
The computer's broken
What a shame.

Suppose I'll get my homework done,
looks like today I'll have
no fun.

Cecilia Hocking (11)
Dunottar School

VOLCANO

The volcano is a rocket,
When it erupts
The lava is hot sweet and sour sauce
That has overflowed,
Bubbling on the cooker.
It wipes out all the plants,
Everything that crawls
And everything you wanted,
Was destroyed by the volcano.

Alexandra Harreiter (11)
Dunottar School

MY CATS

I have a cat named Alfie,
And how sleek is he,
His eyes so wide and bright,
As he steps into the light.

I have a cat named Chloe,
And when we're away,
She looks after Snowy.
She's gentle and kind,
But in the garden,
She's hard to find.

I have a cat named Jim-Bob.
He brings in birds and mice,
Which he thinks are pretty nice.
He loves attention,
But not sure on his reflection.

So I have three cats
As gentle as can be,
Chloe kind,
Alfie sleek
And Jim-Bob, very velvety.

Katy Hill (12)
Dunottar School

I'VE GOT A WITCH

I've got a witch that,
Only comes at night,
She frightens the living daylights,
Out of whoever comes in sight.

She comes to us by broomstick,
With a cat as black as coal,
She wakes me as she tries,
To steal my silver bowl.

I've got a witch who,
Floats above my bed,
Her bulging eyes just stare,
But I don't really care.

I've got a witch,
Who only comes at night.
With a pointed hat and nose and chin,
What a dreadful sight!

I've got a witch
Who rubs her hands with glee,
She cackles quietly,
I think she wants me for her tea.

Then suddenly she stirs.
So I wave goodbye and wish her well,
She wants to cause a fright,
But like my little dog, Sam,
Her bark is worse than her bite.

Claire Shepherd (11)
Dunottar School

My Auntie And The Clock

There is an old house down my road.
Nobody likes to go there as there is a horrible story to be told.

I have heard that clock chime
But only rarely in time and
I know that clock can be bold
Even though it is rather old.

You see it grabbed my auntie from the street
And started whacking her with its feet
Auntie gave a mighty shout
And folk all around came rushing out.

It was a shock to all who saw
Auntie struggling on the floor
I do believe my auntie was saved
By a man to whom she became engaged.

So you see why no one goes
To see the house down our road.

Harriet Jenkins (11)
Dunottar School

The Invitation With No Name

One morning I received in the post,
An invitation while eating my toast.
Quickly I opened it to see what it read,
I jumped up and down on the sofabed.

It's an invitation to a party you see,
I exclaimed with delight *'Yippee, yippee!'*
I jumped in the car and off we went,
Along a lane and down to Kent.

We reached the place, it was a scary house.
With creaking windows and a squealing mouse.
I stepped inside, expecting to see,
A roomful of people waiting for me.

In front of me was a long, dark hall,
'Is anyone there?' I began to call,
Unfortunately to my dismay,
There was no one there so I ran away.

Nicola Hugenholtz (11)
Dunottar School

SPRING TO MIND!

What things spring to mind when you think of Dad?
Smelly socks? A tidy suit? A happy face or sad?

What things spring to mind when you think of Mum?
Pretty dresses or a pretty face that's usually tired but never glum!

What things spring to mind when you think of your big sis?
Heavy music? Fashion victim? A face that's usually full of bliss?

What things spring to mind when you think of your baby bro?
Noisy chap? Likes his toys and has tiny fingers and toes!

And last of all:

What things spring to mind when you think of yourself?
Silly girl? Happy face? Or normal human being?

What things spring to mind when you think of yourself in future times?
Unemployed? Business woman? Or fulfilling your life's dream . . .
         Being a happy human being?

Natasha R S Kay (11)
Dunottar School

WEATHER

The rain is pouring down outside,
And what a noise it makes,
In the garden it makes puddles,
But in the park there are lakes.

The sun is hot but in the wood,
It is so very cool,
I like it here, but not as much,
As in my swimming pool.

The snow is falling everywhere,
It is such a sight,
It covers all the trees and hills,
And everywhere is white.

The wind is raging in the sky,
The storm is at its height,
The room lights up as clear as day,
Although it is the night.

The weather is very strange.
The birds migrate in spring,
It's sometimes hot and sometimes cold,
I wonder what tomorrow will bring?

Elsa King (11)
Dunottar School

THE MOUNTAIN

The mountain top capped with snow,
The trees are waving a silent hello.
A cottage high up in the Alps
The goat boy comes with his yoddles and shouts.

Hear the eagles swoop and cry
See the sunset in the sky.
This is the life on a mountain,
Yes, this is the life on a mountain.

It is spring now,
Boys graze their goats and cows.
The snow is now water and slush,
Whilst flowers grow on every bush.
The animals are born so sweet and dear
While children sing spring is here!

Maxime Sabatini (11)
Dunottar School

FIRST DAY AT SCHOOL

I went to school one day
Without a doubt at all
I listened to the teacher
And said, 'I know it all'
She blinked a little first
Then rose from her chair
'All right my dear come and sit right here'
A tear dropped from one eye
Then she looked at me and said,
'Oh come on dear, it's not half bad
Just think of all those lushy lads.'

Ruth Munroe (11)
Dunottar School

CHOCOLATE

Chocolate's a funny thing,
It's brown, sticky and makes you grin.

It's extremely nice to eat,
It's really sugary and really sweet.

If you hold it in your hand too long,
It melts and tastes all wrong.

When it melts it gets all sticky,
And looks slightly icky!

When you get it on your fingers and toes,
It's amazing just how far it goes.

You can eat chocolate in many ways,
But the one I like the best,
Is putting one piece in my mouth,
And gobbling up the rest!

Georgina Myers (11)
Dunottar School

MY FAMILY

We love our families whatever they do,
Father and Mother too,
Siblings, sisters and brother,
Fight although they love each other.

Grandpa, the dear old thing,
Likes to sit in his armchair and sing,
Grandma's a brilliant cook,
And she likes to read her book.

Auntie is quite arty,
Although she likes to go and party,
Uncle, now he's a laugh,
Once he got his foot stuck in the bath.

I love my family through and through
I would *never* want to have a new.

Tiffini Winn (11)
Dunottar School

SKY AT NIGHT

I looked up at the black sheet,
Hanging above us at night,
And as I looked I thought,
How I'd love to be up there.
And then before I could move,
I felt myself rise and spin,
As fast as light can move,
The stars they spun around me,
Like thousands of little lights,
I passed a huge red ball,
Like a ball of fire.
I kept on spinning,
I saw a yellow ball,
With golden rings around its stomach.
Then I went down.
I felt a bump, everything was still,
And I looked up at the sky at night,
And as I looked up I thought,
How I'd love to be up there.

Helen Rackham (12)
Dunottar School

THE KITTEN

The kitten is a sweet little thing
It is playful and petite
It can chase the leaves and snatch them in mid-air
But when it tastes the leaves it spits them out again.

The kitten can be quite a scamp
Like when it climbs up your curtains
Then down they come like an autumn shower
And you have to wash them again.

But then your sweet kitten suddenly grows up
It doesn't do much clambering about in the house
But then you look outside you will see a funny sight
Which is the choir you hear every night.

But when your lovely cat comes in and sleeps on your nice clean bed
If you saw what your cat's job was you would go crazy
For he is as famous as Beethoven but in cat land
For he is the conductor of the cat choir.

Katherine V Chase (12)
Dunottar School

SNOW

A white blanket falls on the road
Sugar icing settles on the roof
People's footsteps and horses' hooves
Settle on the snow.

Children are laughing
As the snow falls
Children happily play their game
Of snowballs.

A big fat snowman
Stands in the snow.
The children made him fat
With a woolly scarf and a hat.

Rebecca Bendig (12)
Dunottar School

THE VOLCANO AND THE TORNADO

A volcano is a fizzy drink can,
Shaken up inside.
When it foolishly is opened,
Liquid cascades down the sides.

Bubbling out the top and spitting,
In all directions near and far.

They look like fireworks as they burst into space,
Racing down to Earth an exciting chase.

The tornado spins around and around,
Pulling things up making them fly,

A whirling wind, a whooshing sound
Blowing things up and off the ground.

Ruining houses, uprooting trees,
Cars are sucked up in an enormous breeze,
As it approaches everyone flees,

This tornado does not please!

Sophie Robinson (11)
Dunottar School

MY FIRST DAY AT SCHOOL

I was trembling that morning,
I *wouldn't* get out of bed.
I turned on my TV.
'Turn it *off!*' was all Mum said.

She gave me my school uniform
Which wasn't very nice.
Then she said to me, 'Come on dear,
Do I *have* to ask you twice?'

When I had finished dressing,
And had my breakfast too.
I double checked my school bag,
And then put on my shoes.

These things I did quite slowly,
I watched the clock in the hall.
I was going to a new school,
And I wasn't sure at all!

I met my friends at school that day,
They looked as worried as me.
But we all went in together,
That made me very happy.

That day went by so quickly
The lessons were such fun,
I even liked the lunch too
'Can I go tomorrow, Mum?'

Charlotte Surridge (11)
Dunottar School

HARVEST FESTIVAL

Harvest Festival is here again.
Funny we treat it as a game.

We show our love in lovely food,
realising it is no game.

We take for granted every time
the greatest love of our Lord so kind.

People come from miles around
to see the wonders from the ground.

This crop so wonderful and fine
makes us realise time and time.

The greatest care of our Lord above
shines on us with so much love.

Amen.

Daisy Tork (11)
Dunottar School

CHILD

He disappeared one gloomy day,
People said 'He went away.'
No one ever spoke to him,
No one knew his name.
I wish I'd gone and said 'Hello.'
I wish I could have known his name.
He used to sit in that dull corner,
He used to eat his break there
And now that he has gone away,
I seem to miss him more this way.

Katy Shenton (12)
Dunottar School

THE FIRE

Fires are animals,
Stalking their prey.
They start slowly like the smoke,
Very sneaky and away.
Then they suddenly
Are up and ready,
Catching everything they see.
They run up the stairs,
Then quickly down again.

Then when it's over,
The prey is dead.
Everything is quiet and black.
The predator creeps around,
Seeing everything is ruined.
The melted TV and stereo,
All the jewellery gone.
His mother's ring he got to keep,
And other things which had burnt.

Then pleased with himself
He sneaks away.
Full of food of his prey.

Alice Whitney (11)
Dunottar School

THE SEASONS

Spring is joy and happiness,
Babies and creatures
Coming into the world
For the first time.

Summer is holidays,
Spain and France,
It's for families
Who don't get time to get
Together.

Autumn is falling leaves,
Browns and reds
Falling from a distance
To the ground,
The animals are getting ready
For their wintry hardship.

Winter is cold but families
Keep each other warm,
Giving them presents of love.
They also get ready
For the New Year to come.
Cheering and saying
'Hip hip hurray!

Marie-Claire Wyatt (12)
Dunottar School

THE BOX

There is a box under the bed,
I am desperate to know what's within.
My curiosity is driving me mad,
The constant temptation to look in.

It is all I can think of, day and night,
It is as though it is inside my head.
The picture of the box,
Sitting under the bed.

It is brown and square,
An ordinary box just sitting there.
Its mystery fascinates me,
But I am unable to find the key,
That will unlock the secret within.

Helen Crawford (12)
Dunottar School

LIFE

Life is like a caterpillar
Life doesn't change for a while
Life is full of good things
Leaves and cabbages
Life appears to end at the chrysalis
Although it looks dead,
Life thrives
A butterfly
Flying away
A new and beautiful image
Life after death.

Sarah Andrews (13)
Dunottar School

HIGH IN THE MOUNTAINS

High in the mountains
Where I wish to be,
My heart calls me back
To the aspen trees.

To the swift flowing rivers,
Cold and crystal clear,
The blue peaks of the mountains,
That I wish to be near.

Hummingbirds flitter
From flower to flower,
Eagles soar high
Birds of power.

No commitments
Time drifting by,
I have no connection
With the world outside.

No care in the world
Taking things as they come,
Close to the heavens
Under the sun.

Heather Caddick (12)
Dunottar School

FAMILY AND FRIENDS

Family and friends are always there,
Ready to share your happy times
And help you through your troubles
When you're feeling down.

Easily they can succeed
Never leaving you upset and
Down.
Sharing and caring family and friends.

They're always on the go,
Never are they slow to realise
When you are unhappy.
Quickly they come to the rescue
And help us through our troubles.

Mending our unhappiness,
So that we are not alone
And isolated, they care
And love us lots.

You're lucky if you have family and friends
Just like I do,
To help you through.
And one day hopefully
You will do the same thing too.

Michelle Chasey (12)
Dunottar School

THE SEASONS

Summer, spring, autumn and winter -
The four seasons of the year.
They always argue about who's best
And who comes up at the rear.

'I'm the nicest!' declared summer.
'You see, I keep people warm.
The flowers bloom all the season
And the bees come in swarms.'

'I'm the coolest month!' scowled winter.
'I let people have fun!
All the world is covered in sheets
Of white snow for everyone.'

'Look who's talking!' laughed autumn.
'With me, the trees go bare!
Fruits blossom and ripen
And there are leaves everywhere.'

Spring had remained quiet all this time
While the others were arguing.
She watched summer, autumn and winter
Talk about what they bring.

'For heaven's sake! *Stop arguing!'*
Spring said, 'You're all such a bore!
Keep quiet for the the rest of the day -
Because I can't take it anymore!'

Raeesa Chowdhury (12)
Dunottar School

THE LAKE DISTRICT

The Lake District is a silent tranquil place,
Full of beautiful scenery.

Miles of long fields with high trees.
Trees so high you can see the leaves silhouetted against the sky.

Lonely sheep grazing in tarns and valleys.

Small slate cottages resting in the hills,
With warm burning fires.

The lakes like mirrors,
From flowing streams.

Suddenly shattered,
By a high-powered speedboat,
With reckless drivers.

The Lake District will be somewhere to look at in my dreams.

Emma Halsall (12)
Dunottar School

THE EARLY MORNING

In the glistening hours of the morning sun,
Songs of birds fill the air
With sounds of summertime,
So bright and so warm.

I jump out of bed,
And pull back the curtains.
I peer out the window,
The dew is still wet on the grass.

The sun is just coming up,
Over the top of the trees.
Everything looks peaceful,
The sky looks dazzling red.

As the silhouettes of a flock of birds appear in the distance,
They look like black lines.
Of changing patterns,
In the scarlet sky.

Ashleigh Cheall (12)
Dunottar School

THE DENTIST

Jane had a pain
In her mouth
It felt like a chisel
Digging in her gum.

'Oh what a shame, shame, shame
Oh what a pain'
Said Jane.

The dentist found her
Cavity,
As the chair defined
Gravity.

'Has the pain gone now, Jane?
Give the receptionist all your loose change,
Change, change
All your loose change.'

Alice Chilton (12)
Dunottar School

A THOUSAND YEARS

First came the Stone Age, the most basic of all,
Then the Bronze and Iron in turn had their fall.
For along came the Romans with armour and swords.
Then the Anglo-Saxons, Vikings, my word they were hordes.
Soon came the Normans with horses for war,
Then the Middle ages: men hunted wild boar,
Tudors and Stuarts were next on the line,
Then Georgians and Victorians fitted in fine.
The two world wars were closely related.
Then onto us: some say we are hated,
But our lives are not quite as traumatic.
We just seem to enjoy being dramatic!
Soon we'll be celebrating the millennium's end
So we can look back at what to amend.

Harriet Ferguson (12)
Dunottar School

HAPPINESS

Laughter awakes me on this day,
I feel significant in every way.

I love myself and am glad to be alive,
Just like royalty is about to arrive.

Tears approach my eyes,
As sadness dies.

Fears and worries are totally out,
And life becomes great, without a doubt!

Sonia Goodman (12)
Dunottar School

THE DREAM TREE

As I walked along the boughs of the tree
The upside down cat stared at me.
The python slithered into the frothing foams
And the tiger stared at the silent gnomes.
The dark pink lake rippled and curled
The tortured in the dungeon roared.
The witch's den seemed to shake
In a far away unearthly earthquake.
The wizard's books formed an arrow
Pointing to the dog sparrow.
As I climbed higher up the tree
Coconuts shoot and fell on me.
The deep blue sea's waves rose and fell
The deserted beaches remained still.
The old leaves fell and browned
As I came down, down, down . . .

Charlotte Mann (13)
Dunottar School

JIGSAW

A missing piece,
From my life,
A friend perhaps,
Or maybe a love,
Just one piece,
Is missing,
From this jigsaw,
Of my life . . .

Emily Stanford (12)
Dunottar School

GOBBLE

As the family gets ready for bed the gobble is ready to play
But what the gobble does not know is that Mother is getting a drink
The gobble crawls into the kitchen unseen then makes a dash
for the fridge
Except Mother is there with her drink, she screams and drops her glass
And runs around the kitchen in fear
The gobble on the other hand has his face in a cake
And looks as if he had just put his head into a muddy puddle
The smell of the gobble permeates the room and it smells like egg
But the gobble has run away and has gone to make someone else's
kitchen smell that way.

Amy Harmer (13)
Dunottar School

THE WILD PONIES

The wild ponies that run so free,
With flowing tail and flying mane,
Wide nostrils, never stretched by pain.
Mouths bloodless to the bit or rein
And feet that iron never shod
And flanks unscarred by the spur or rod.

A thousand horses - the wild - the free,
Like waves that roll over the sea,
Came thickly thundering on!

Charlotte Alexandra Souster (12)
Dunottar School

MY GRANDAD'S DREAM

In his bed my grandad lay,
His face a pale mixture
Of a dull yellow and white.
His bones were aching with arthritis,
His body fragile, thin and light.
His hair was but a few grey wisps,
His teeth yellow and crackled.
But his eyes,
Those deep, deep blue eyes
Stayed ever mysterious that night.

As my grandad lay there,
He dreamed of how he used to be free,
Of how he used to skip and run
And think of what he would be.
Of how he could play sport and games,
Without that dreadful feeling
Of being
Meaningless, useless and lame.

Later on in the night my grandad softly slipped away.
Happily dreaming
Of the fine old day
And although his body was dead,
His spirit was happy and free.
But those deep, deep blue eyes
Were shut forever more.

Melissa Rambridge (12)
Dunottar School

THE LION CUB

As the cub approached me stumbling,
He fell at my feet.
Bantam and cute,
Like a newborn puppy.
His crystal clear blue eyes were shimmering
In front of me,
The colour of its coat was a creamy beige,
The shade of a misty sea shell
Sprinkled with sand.
When I touched the cub
He felt so malleable and cuddly,
Just like a teddy bear.
His razor blade teeth were gleaming white,
With a long salivating tongue!
As I knelt down to pick him up,
He pounced into my arms
And gave me a hug.

Mikaela Mills (12)
Dunottar School

JACE

There once was a boy called Jace,
He made fun of his sister Grace,
Grace walked up,
With her silly little pup,
And smacked him on the head with her brace.

Jace wasn't about to stop the tease,
About Grace's very fat knees,
Grace was sad,
So the boys were glad.
And she flung him into some trees.

Grace was getting told off a lot,
Because of kicking Jace's bot,
But she didn't care,
It was becoming unfair,
So she pushed him down in a cot.

Charlotte Haydon (12)
Dunottar School

ORANGES AND LEMONS

Oranges and lemons,
Sweet and sour,
Their rich juices flow.
A purpose is theirs
As they go, never to be seen again.
An orange is a thing of great beauty
It shares its sweetness with others
And is thought of highly.
A lemon,
He has a bewildering bitterness
Yet others value him richly
And he is a thing of many arts
He is never without
And proclaims a sense of wondrous glory
Which he gives,
And never refuses
To the people of the dark,
And sometimes his song embodies
Something which is neither right
Nor wrong.

Lucinda Lane (12)
Dunottar School

SADNESS

Sadness is the colour of tears,
The feeling of the changing years.

Through times of joy it's always near,
Like an ever and ongoing fear.

Sadness never reigns supreme,
But when it comes, it shatters every dream.

Sadness never comes and goes,
But always exists, a multitude of woes.

Yes sadness is the colour of tears,
The feeling through those changing years!

Helen Hudson (12)
Dunottar School

THE NEW FOREST

Out on the moor I gallop so free,
The grass so green,
The sky seems to beam,
I love the New Forest, because it's my dream.

The thunder, the lightning,
The rain on my face,
Clip clopping quicker into a race,
The horses beside me and
The horses in front,
The New Forest is a wonderful place!

Lauren Parsons (12)
Dunottar School

THE WOMAN OF THE WORLD

Winter trees sway, swirl
As the wind blows, cold
So the leaves get caught,
In her long, brown hair.

As her breath goes white
And she wheezes from a chest,
That is silently dying,
From too many cold nights

And her eyes are dull,
And her fingers are numb,
And her cheeks are pale,
And her words are sad.

She doesn't care anymore.
Since she has nothing.
She doesn't know anymore.
She took too much for granted.

She has no warmth left,
She has no calm left,
She threw it all away -
Long, long, ago.

The lady of the leftovers,
That are now her life.
Just because she is a tramp,
Everyone is cold.
The woman of the world.

Jocasta Jones (12)
Dunottar School

MY DREAM

As I walk into my English class,
My mind drifts elsewhere.
To a bright, sunny, tropical island.
Fancy flowers in my hair.

As I bathe in the cool waters
The birds sing, the waves lap.
As I lie upon the golden sands
The branches in the breeze softly flap.

I wander in a forest dark
With many an animal darting.
I love to see this wonderful world
But the fun is only starting.

A cloud lifts me up and carries me
Over the land and sea.
I'm walking on air today, my friends,
I'm shouting out loud with glee.

The teacher taps on the desk
And accuses me of dreaming.
I wake up with a jump and a start,
I *was* dreaming, it is seeming.

Amelia Lewis (12)
Dunottar School

CHRISTMAS

The candles are lit
The fires are on
The roast is cooking
Dinner's on

Rosey is playing
She's only two
Her present is a toy zoo

Jim is five
Getting tall
Mum and Dad got him Star Wars Four

Mum is cooking
Working hard
Timing out the vege parts

Dad is helping with the roast
Carving turkey in the kitchen

What a perfect Christmas Day
With all my family
For our Christmas meal
That happens only once a year
And with it brings good cheer.

Kate Marshall (12)
Dunottar School

IMAGINATION

As the winter draws in
And the fires are lit,
The show begins
And a dragon of massive proportions
Comes leaping out,
Breathing a fire flame,
Between the black mountains of coal.

As I begin to be engulfed
By this beast,
The scene changes
And it is now a battlefield,
With sparks flying out
As gun explosions,
Coming from behind,
The same black mountains.

As it calms,
The finale begins,
With dancers swaying
Swiftly around the stage
And as a finishing, a slow bow,
Dying down leaving a pile
Of the old black mountains.

Amanda Rea (13)
Dunottar School

THE FAMILY OF FURBIES

There was a family of Furbies,
Who lived in the town of Burbies.
Their eyes were all blue,
Their toe nails were too
And this family was called the Wurbies.

There was a bright pink Furby,
His parents called him Zurby.
His ears were vain,
Oh he was such a pain
And his sister called him Durby.

There was a lime green Furby,
Her family called her Curby.
Her nose was so long,
You could use it as a gong.
Everyone called her just Nosey.

There was a sky-blue Furby,
Her children called her Gurby.
She was the mother,
She had a brother.
A brother who lived in Murby.

There was a rose red Furby,
His children called him Turby.
He was the dad,
Once a young lad.
Who went to live in Derby.

Sarah Turner (12)
Dunottar School

THE FUTURISTIC CREATURE!

What if the millennium was a creature?
What a strange feature!
Would he have one eye!
Maybe a light bulb or a star from the sky!
Would his nose be like a socket
And his mouth a pocket,
With his words across it, like a screen!
A computer for a body!
Cables and pylons for arms and legs,
Plugs for hands and for ears!
His brain a microchip that functions on his food!
His food, is all the electricity that he can find!
He gobbles all these electronic functions up to restore energy to live!

Would he be a disaster,
Or a futuristic master?
Who can tell?
We will see!
What the *millennium* will turn out to be!

Fiona Small (12)
Dunottar School

THE CIRCUS

Acrobats leaping,
Cream and custard pies.
Performing dogs and lions,
In front of my eyes.

Clowns with white faces
And the ringmaster bold.
Dressed from head to toe,
In scarlet and gold.

Ice-cream and candyfloss,
Flags to buy and wave.
Trapeze artists swooping,
They are so brave.

How I love the circus,
It is such fun.
Come and buy a ticket,
There's something for everyone.

Pamela Jayne Stallard (12)
Dunottar School

I LOVE EVERYTHING ABOUT YOU...

She looked in the mirror and smiled,
Those eyes, those deep green eyes that smile.
Her dimples, the dimples I love on each cheek side,
The dimples, she always tries to hide.
Her skin, pure as a virgin bride.
Her lips the way they curve when she smiles
And her little button nose, the one she said
Taught her everything she knows.
And now there she lies years on, still as stone,
But still with those eyes, those deep green eyes.
The dimples I love and she hates . . .
Well she did.
Her skin still pure but with a slight sign of ageing.
Her lips still curved and her little button nose,
The nose that taught her everything she knows.

Becky Watts (12)
Dunottar School

HOLLY

A flash of lightning scarred down her face,
her ears are long and alert,
liver chestnut is the colour of her coat.
Her eyes like onyx.
Her hooves like ivory.
She is any riders dream.
She is as comfortable to ride as sitting
on a rocking chair.
When she's happy her eyes are like an eclipse,
she moves as if she were gliding on ice.
Her mane cascades over her silky brown neck.
She is just like Holly, smooth on one side,
sharp on the other.

Charlotte Venables (12)
Dunottar School

CLOUDS

A jellyfish up in the sky,
A silent ghost goes floating by,
A giant quietly smiles at you,
A witch huddled over a pot of stew,
A bird attacks an overgrown rat,
An old lady strokes her greying cat.
A shadow cast across the sky,
The winds begin to moan and sigh,
A black panther is stalking near,
Her soft growling you begin to hear,
A clap of thunder, lightning flash,
You look around and then you see,
Clouds can be anything you want them to be.

Virginia Stacey (13)
Dunottar School

MY DREAM

When I dream,
It is of a countryside theme.
There are many small, rolling hills
And dark, dark woods,
That give you the chills.
There are slow running brooks
And high up in the trees,
There is the caw of the rooks.
There are many green trees and bushes,
Full of assorted berries
And in a copse
There are tales of magical fairies.
The well harvested fields,
Seem to glisten in the sunlight
And at night there is the fireflies' light.
In the morning the rabbits
Come to eat the grass.
But at night, they run from
The foxes very fast!
At sunset you can hear the sweet birds' chirp
And the silhouettes of the leaves in the
Autumn breeze seem to flirt.

Elizabeth Stansfeld (13)
Dunottar School

INSPIRATION

I need inspiration!
And I cannot find any.
My mind's gone blank
And I cannot think.
What is the matter with me?
Where are all the ideas I usually have?
I think and think
Still nothing.
Nothing excites me.
Nothing feels right.
I have searched and searched and failed to find it.
Not a flicker.
Not a spark.
Just one good idea to light up the dark
Is all I need.
It's here somewhere I know it.
And I will find it eventually
But for now,
I sit and wait
For inspiration to find me.

Stephanie Wells (12)
Dunottar School

YEARS TO COME!

I believe there are no cars and no pollution too
Just skateboards for me and you.
I believe there's no supermarkets just mobile phones,
I think people like staying at their homes.

Get your shopping list, type it on a PC,
The food comes to you and you fill with glee.
Imagine robot people, they will never leave you alone,
They follow you to the shop and then follow you home.

Bobbi Hutchinson (11)
Reigate School

WHAT WILL MY VOICE BE LIKE?

What will my voice be like?
What will my voice be like?
Will it be soft and quiet,
Or strong and loud?
What will my voice be like?

What will I be like?
What will I be like?
Will I be shy or not,
Or funny or not?
What will I be like?

When will I learn?
When will I learn?
When I'm 5 or 6,
Or maybe never?
When will I learn?

When will I die?
When will I die?
68 or 33,
Or maybe alive forever.
When will I die?

Shelana Peerbeccus (11)
Reigate School

FUTURE VOICES

In my dreams I heard a voice, a deep voice that sounded so familiar
to me.

Who's that?
It's you when you're 21
But I am only 11, I still have 10 years to wait
But I am in the future, I am a future voice, an illusion
Can I ask you questions?
Yes, but I can't answer all of them
Why?
Because if I tell you everything your life will be too easy
and not a challenge
He was exciting and mysterious, he was in my dreams
Could he be true?
What do I need to know? Oh! I've got it, my exam results
OK, you will get English and maths, I will start with maths,
You will get . . .

'Christopher, Christopher, it's time to get up' whispered my mum.

Christopher Burr (11)
Reigate School

FUTURE VOICES

I hear some voices calling out to me, ringing at my name,
I hear my conscience and my dreams,
I get so bored that I scream.

I see babies crying,
Then grown-ups fighting, I just don't know what's going on.
I get so confused that then I have a déjà vu
and then I'm sitting down talking.

I see dreams that seem so real I seem like a fortune teller,
I imagine things before they happen,
I hear things that no one hears,
My conscience reads to me like a book,
I really am a fortune teller!

Maxine Cronin (11)
Reigate School

FUTURE VOICES

I hear a voice,
It's not mine,
Now my conscience has crossed the line.
Incessant talking,
Babbling on,
Trying to tell me I'm doing wrong.
I refuse to listen
And block my ears,
I shall not hear a word it says.
All at once
He's standing there,
Hands on hips and an angry stare.
Dad's model car,
His pride and joy,
I'd been told it wasn't a toy.
It fell to pieces,
Did I feel bad,
When I turned and saw my dad?
The voice was right
And I was wrong,
Guess I should have listened all along.

George Bateman (11)
Reigate School

FUTURE VOICES

What will happen in the future, will it be like today?
Are the answers around me, in some strange and chilling way?
The flashes of images that go through my mind confuse me,
Yet through them somehow I find,
Some resemblance of order for the things I have known,
Like people and places I may have called home.
But then in a moment, just out of the blue,
They change into things that are totally new.
Like pictures of things I could never have seen,
Like people and places, I have never been.
The rumble of voices though distant I hear,
Convince me that now I have nothing to fear.
When closing my eyes are the visions I see,
My past, my future or just reality.

Simon West (11)
Reigate School

FUTURE

The future

F ade, fantastic, fabulous, factual, final, failure, fat, fall-out.
U nusual, unused, unfamiliar, user-friendly.
T echnical, temperature, terminal, thermal.
U nknown.
R ecycle, rubbish,
E nvironmentally friendly, environment.

The future.

Samantha May (13)
Reigate School

FUTURE, AN ILL WORLD

The days came and went
With the sounds of death and destruction on every part
Of the Earth's wintry core
Civilisation had been bent
The world was feeling sore

In many a year vegetation had not been seen
And the trees were no more
This was down to the sun's fatal beam
But no one was no one so no one knew no more

The world had gone to bed
Science had taken control
People started to mourn for the dead
It was about time this world was given parole

The inventions poured through
But they were all passed out
People didn't have a clue
This world was about to lose its championship bout

But now here we are
On a planet afar
Our world was killed
Because we did not clear what we spilled.

Alistair Bance (13)
Reigate School

FUTURE VOICES SPEAK

We hear them,
When they call us.
They hear me,
When I don't even speak.
The difference is,
They understand us.
Everything we know,
Has already happened for them.
They can show us images and visions,
If we would only look.
There will be so much,
To touch and taste and smell.
It will be unbelievable,
To our feelings and soul.
They have been enlightened
And given a sixth sense.
Only the future voices,
Can bring us from the past.

Helen Kulka (13)
Reigate School

FUTURE VOICES - FUTURE DEATHS

Voices,
Calling, screaming,
Roaring, roaring nonsense,
The world stops like a battery dead clock.

Future voices calling,
Calling Red Death,
Upon whom who disobeys me?
Me, you it echoes,
Future Deaths.

Shrieking voices shout run,
They all follow like lemmings,
I run to seek he who is threatening me,
Nothing but a cloud sucking me in,
In, in, sucking me in, in, in.

Sam Wheeler (11)
Reigate School

FUTURE VOICES

Fortune teller, fortune teller,
When will I die?
Fortune teller, fortune teller,
Please don't lie.
Fortune teller, fortune teller,
Will I become rich?
Fortune teller, fortune teller,
Will I fall in a ditch?
Fortune teller, fortune teller,
Will the world end?
Fortune teller, fortune teller,
On who can I depend?
Fortune teller, fortune teller,
Is that an alien I see?
Fortune teller, fortune teller,
Has it come to take me?
Fortune teller, fortune teller,
What can you see?
Will the world disappear
In the ever growing sea?

Laura Batten (11)
Reigate School

THE FUTURE

Future is a puzzling thing,
It happens every day,
Tomorrow will be over soon,
And yesterday will be gone.
You never know what's going to happen,
Bam! It could be you!
So I would stay quite near to home
And just watch what you do.
Spaceships - nwooan! as they zoom past,
Could be the next form of transport.
So get your spaceship licence now,
Or you'll be left behind.
I want to fly to Venus,
I want to fly to Mars,
But all the planes have been booked up
And I was not too fast.
So the future is a puzzling thing,
It happens every day.
Just be careful how you go
And just remember the future holds your life!

Sarah Batchelor (13)
Reigate School

FUTURE VOICES

Here I am, old and grey,
My favourite place, where I must lay,
Thinking back from a while ago,
I miss my youth and the golden glow.

If only now, I was young,
My life would be, not as fun,
All around me there is smoke,
In the skies and where I look.

Lots of buildings, one hundred feet,
Traffic jams, in every street,
The kids these days with alcohol,
I see it when I'm out for a stroll.

Yes, there is a lot of green,
With litter on, nothing is clean.

Sam Causon (13)
Reigate School

FUTURE VOICES' WARNING

Dark corrupted skylines,
Black poisonous air,
Which looks, tastes and smells like floating tar.
No water is clean,
No grass green,
All is tinged with blackness,
Even the natural spirits.
Evil lurks around every corner,
In the form of mutated corpses.
The future, it seems, is not a place to be.

Buildings are tarnished,
The ground diseased,
Both are old, neither are painless.
No waste is binned,
No paper recycled,
All is bleak and horrifying,
Even trees hang limp.
Good is a legend,
Gone forever.
The future, it seems, it not a place to be.

Alan Thomas (13)
Reigate School

FUTURE VOICES

1999

I used to live on a housing estate,
They came and knocked it down,
Grotty old housing estates
Deserve to be knocked down.

2000

In place of my Victorian house
They have put a modern replica,
Fussy old-fashioned houses gone,
Modern look-alike replacements.

2001

I used to shop in a shopping centre
But now it's all done by net.
No more walking around,
Take orders, they arrive the next day.

2005

I don't have a pen any more,
Instead I spend my time typing.
Messy ink pens get everywhere,
Now words are a lot neater.

2007

My only joy gone for now,
Books have vanished forever,
Books only take up space,
Play on the computer instead.

2010

Everything is computerised,
The Millennium Bug has taken over,
Oh the joy, everything is mine,
I rule the world.

Helena Humpherson (11)
Reigate School

THE FUTURE IN SPACE

The future, the future,
What will it hold?
The future, the future,
What will be told?

Talking cars and motorbikes,
Having a meteor race,
Or just the current theory of
Aliens from outer space.

Will we be living on the other planets?
The moon or even the sun.
Whatever happens in the future,
It sounds like lots of fun!

Scientists are studying,
What we call far away
But in the future
We won't have to work but play!

Why worry about Nostradmus' theory,
The world won't end too soon,
And when it does, if ever it will,
We'll be living on the moon!

Laura Nye (13)
Reigate School

WHAT FUTURE HAVE I GOT?

Queen Victoria reigned when I was born.
I've seen two world wars begin and end.
Adolf Hitler, Winston Churchill.
John Kennedy and Martin Luther King.
The atomic bomb drop on Hiroshima.
Neil Armstrong walk on the moon.
Prime ministers and presidents come and go.
Six different monarchs ruling Britain.
The fall of the Berlin Wall and communism.
Third World starvation, AIDs and drugs.
I've raised four children and watched them grow.
Watched them leave and move away.
I've buried my husband and faced life alone.
I'm 99 years old - what future have I got?
The dawn of a new millennium.
My telegram from the Queen.
Freezing cold, scared to turn the heating on.
Hypothermia or higher bills.
Losing my hearing and eyesight.
Losing my mobility and my independence.
Losing my friends, missing my family.
Waiting for a hip replacement operation.
Waiting for a place at the old folks' home.
Meals on wheels, the occasional game of bingo.
Going to another friend's funeral.
I've survived for nearly a century.
What future have I got?

Lisa Glossop (13)
Reigate School

FUTURISTIC GENERATIONS

The other night I had a dream,
that all children will be treated equally,
all homeless will have a home,
all sick will have a cure,
there will be no crime, no murders,
just peace and tranquillity.

The other night I had a dream,
that all animals will roam the Earth,
no extinction, no hurting and no deaths,
every animal will be treated like humans, equally,
there will be no such thing as deforestation,
just peace and tranquillity.

The other night I had a dream,
the Earth will be clean,
the air will be pure,
no cars shooting out pollution,
there will be no cleaner place than Earth,
just peace and tranquillity.

The other night I had a dream,
that everything we do will be operated by remote,
computers will order and deliver food,
every car will not have a window,
just a hologram on the screen of where you are going,
just peace and tranquillity.

The other night I had a dream
that all this will come true.

Jennifer Briggs (13)
Reigate School

FUTURE VOICES

I am the future,
I am your future.
Do what you will with me,
You are too late to save the trees.
The ozone layer wastes by day
And the Earth's resources fade away.

You cover all the land with stone,
Those who are left will stand alone.
You make guns and bombs to kill us all,
Soon the blood will fill the hall.
The icebergs have already melted,
All the minerals have smelted.

I am the future,
I am your future.
Do what you will with me.
I am dying, help me,
The Earth is withering and meek,
I am the future, the future is bleak.

Genevieve Noble (13)
Reigate School

FUTURE WORLD

The millennium is only days away
And everyone's celebrating
And everyone's trying to improve the world
For our children's children to live in.

The world will be saved from pollution
The world will be saved from hate
The world will be saved in every way we can
For our children's children to live in.

The world will be freed from starvation
The world will be freed from war
The world will be freed in every way we can
For our children's children to live in.

The world will be helped financially
The world will be freed from debt.
The world will be saved in every way we can
For our children's children to live in.

Emma Williams (12)
Reigate School

MAGIC MILLENNIUM?

Are you pessimistic about the pollution problem
                                    panicking the politicians?
Are you concerned about conservation, criminals killing cute creatures?
Are you fretting over fertiliser fiddling with the future of
                                    the eco-system?
Are you grieving over GM foods muddling with
                                    genetic groups of genes?
Are you bothered about the bug bodging up your business network?
Are you worried about global warming wrecking the
                                    winter and making it warmer?

The Millennium Dome,
The London Eye,
Scaling the London skyline.
Costing millions of pounds,
Making the headlines all for one millennium.

Is the future going to be fantastic or a failure?
I'll let you decide.

Joe Costin (12)
Reigate School

FUTURE VOICES

As I stand here,
In this cold and empty field,
With my mask over my face,
I remember what it used to be like,
Hot and wet, and full of life
But some humans had to take it.
They did not care what it would do.
Wiping out wildlife forever.
I hear the guns around me,
I see the tear stained face,
Of a little girl with half an arm,
Because of the greedy human race.
When they started all this trouble,
They didn't bother to listen.
They did not listen to the future voices,
They did not listen to us.

Samantha Tyrrell (13)
Reigate School

ME IN THE FUTURE

In the future I will be old and wrinkly,
I would probably be around about fifty!
Electronic clothes that get to a temperature,
By the touch of a button is what you want.
Really cool cars that change their colour,
You just touch a button. . . bleep! Pink to royal blue.
We would have flying carpets that fly to the moon,
We're heading there now, we'll be there soon!

Joanne Pedley (11)
Reigate School

SCHOOL

Our teachers are all aliens,
We can't mess about,
Because they have millions of eyes
And they all bulge out,
It is brilliant at lunch time,
We go down to the games room
And there we have time out,
The dinner hall is brilliant,
We don't have to wait,
All we do is push buttons
And our waiter brings it to us,
The same applies for drinks as well,
We don't have deafening bells
We have an ear piece
That only you can hear,
We place it in our ear
And that's our school in the future.

David Cadwallader (11)
Reigate School

WHAT WILL COME NEXT?

Robots are being programmed,
Music is becoming weirder,
Soon there will be flying cars and life on Mars,
Rocket aeroplanes shooting around,
Computer communications becoming reality,
Nostalgia going through your head,
Television voices are changing like the weather,
Inventions are our lives,
Millennium Domes what will come next.

Kathryn Blake (12)
Reigate School

WHAT DOES THE FUTURE HOLD?

What does the future hold?
What are we all destined for?
Will the world be blown up by a nuclear war?
Who will be leading us in the future?
Why do we have future?
Where do we go when we die?
Why do we have time?
Will we all die on the millennium's first day?
Why do we have life?
Will we all become aliens?
Who will be our new queen?
What does the future hold?

Elise Reason (14)
Reigate School

FUTURE VOICES

Lions and tigers are extinct, all gone,
The supermarkets have become one big con
But King Harry has made people drive solar cars,
We have even found microscopic life on Mars.
Houses have become a thing of elegance and beauty,
Children's eating is a lot more healthy.
More and more beggars are getting a home,
Whilst London have replaced the Millennium Dome.
Old people no longer have to live on their own,
Secrets of our planet are now known.

Daniel Allen (12)
Reigate School

MILLENNIUM

In the future we have electric cars,
Ones that can shoot up way past Mars.
Basically everything will be electric,
Even your grandpa's stick.
School will be excellent when you go there,
Doing your work in a leather chair.
At lunch time you can play whatever sport,
Even if it's golf in a netball court.
The environment will be wicked greens and browns,
With sweet birds singing making loving sounds.
No, it won't be stupid with alligators on the loose,
Not lions or tigers or even a moose.
Your house will be enormous with electric stairs,
With a mall-sized bedroom filled with cuddly bears.
In your back garden you'll have a football stadium,
Or you could have your own palladium!
The food is really yummy, it's great,
You can have it in two seconds on your plate.
It is a powder contained in a small packet,
All you need to do is open it up and empty it.
That's the end of my talk, now I have to go,
I'll see you soon in the future though.
Just look for the future in the sky,
But now it's time to say goodbye.

David Waring (12)
Reigate School

FUTURE VOICES

My voice is telling me about the future
I can see a vivid picture
Little babies driving cars
Little girls with bubbly spa
Everything's changed from when I was young
Nothing around the streets that smells of dung
New technology is dazzling my mind
I try to fit in, everyone's kind
Umbrellas are not in use anymore,
Might it start raining? The weather is poor.
People on the streets are all happy
And there is no longer any dog food called *Chappy*.
Reading football club is really good
Tranmere would get to the Premiership, if they could.
Italy have won the World Cup the most
England and Brazil can no longer boast.
Some new invented robots deliver the post.

Alan Robb (12)
Reigate School

THE NEW FUTURE

We will be replaced in years to come,
New days, new lives, new future,
It looked at our lives alone, at one,
Ready to take over and finally be free.

They stared at us like food ready to eat,
Or drink us down in one go
Their voices rumbled like lightning about to burst
Screaming, shouting, having to obey.

Trees ripped out of the ground
Roof tops shattered in the wind
Louder, louder, like a train coming closer
When voices say 'Future, dark, alone, undiscovered.'

Happy lives faded away,
Great experiences faded away
Hundreds of years they've wanted to take over
Now it's all the forgotten past.

Louise Catt (11)
Reigate School

FUTURE VOICES SPEAKING

Future voices
Uttering, muttering,
Mumbling, grumbling.

Future voices, telling us
The pleasure, the pain
The terror
Giving us a name.

Future voices
Warning us,
Advising us.

Future voices
Telling us secrets
Telling us of revolutions
Inventions, discoveries.

Future voices giving us
An earache!

Matthew Izard (11)
Reigate School

FUTURE VOICES

It's not like the olden days,
We've hardly got any money.
Life is so boring
And it is not at all funny.
Pollution has got worst in the years
GM crops have taken over nature.
This goes against all the rules
And is not the vision of the creator
Life has gone full circle.
With my faculties leaving.
I'm sure I enter the fires of hell.
Judgement day is here, screaming.

Brett Avery (12)
Reigate School

2084

The third millennium is drawing near.
The government is watching you is all we hear.
We travel from place to place on solar powered scooters.
It is dangerous as people speed and they don't use their hooters.
Our healthy food is grown indoors using sprinklers and lights.
The good things are that we're friendly and that nobody fights.
We all live indoors in giant glass domes.
But we can never talk freely as the government bugs our homes.
The world outside is red and bare
And we daren't go out because of the poisoned air.
So people of your time, act now before it is too late.
Act now to stop your planet being ruined, at a later date.

Morgan James (12)
Reigate School

TWO THOUSAND AND SEVENTY NINE

It is the year two thousand and seventy nine,
In my ninety third year I look back in time,
They've cured cancer, diabetes and AIDS,
Drugs are outlawed, no need for raids.

There's plenty of food for everyone,
There's lots of clean water for those in the sun,
No one is hungry, the famine has gone,
There is no war, we do no wrong.

The factories are no longer here,
The o-zone is safe, there's no need to fear,
The seas are not plagued, dumping is banned,
The oceans are clean, so is the sand.

This is why I'm content at last,
There is love and peace unlike the past.

Charlotte Lucas (13)
Reigate School

MY PLANET YEARS FROM NOW

When the world explodes I will float up into space,
I will land on a planet with many other people,
The planet has not yet been discovered,
There will be animals that come alive that have been extinct
None of the people on the planet will need oxygen,
It will snow every winter and be sunny every summer,
There will be no zoos to lock up animals,
My planet will be like ours with more trees,
All children will get three days off school,
That's my planet years from now.

Lauren Best (11)
Reigate School

FUTURE VOICES

I warned you about this.
I told you not to,
I told you this would happen.
You will never learn.
You used it all up
There is none left.
It will never be back again.
The whole world has changed
This used to be a beautiful place!
Flowers blooming and friendly people meeting,
But look at it now,
There's too much pollution and violence about!
Just think about what you've done!
I have told you before
But did you listen!
No!

Katie Smith (12)
Reigate School

COMPUTERS

Computers said the past,
Were really new,
Everybody wanted one, everybody wanted one,
They will be the future, said the past,
They will be the future!

Computers said the present,
Everybody wants one, everyone wants one,
Games, the internet, e-mail and fun,
They will be the future said the present,
They will be the future!

Computers said the future,
Everybody's got one, nobody needs one,
They were the future said the future,
Now they are the past!

Joanne Dalley (11)
Reigate School

MY WORLD

It was like the whole world shook
when I heard these voices,
the whole universe went silent waiting
for the noise.
Babies stopped screaming,
children stopped playing
and that's when it happened the voices returned.
The voices spoke about the future,
telling us how it would be.
They spoke out loud about the houses,
saying that we would not live there.
The voices laughed about us people,
they said we would not be needed.
They carried on and yelled out like
we would get scared,
about the invasion to wipe us all out
and that's where it ended, the laughs and
the screams,
everyone stared and will never remember.
But I and some people will never forget,
we will be ready for the mystery invasion.

Sophie Upfold (11)
Reigate School

STOP!

Stop said the future,
A lollipop lady in the road.
Stop said the future,
A man teaching a class.

What I asked the future,
A question beyond my mind.
What I asked the future,
A puzzled old lady in front of a fire.

Why I asked the future,
A small child asking her mum.
Why I asked the future,
Please tell me what's wrong?

I have said the future,
I'll tell you once more,
I have said the future
But I'll tell you again.

Inventions said the future,
They'll all be replaced!
Inventions said the future,
And so will you.

Your life said the future,
It'll all go wrong!
Your life said the future
It'll all backfire.

Stephanie Seal (11)
Reigate School

FUTURE WORLD

Bridges of courage,
Rivers of faith,
Mountains of perseverance,
Give and not take.

Oceans of friendship,
Caverns of love,
Skies of pure happiness,
Rainbows above

But in a dark corner,
Of this wonderful place,
There lives a dark Hobbit
With a frown on his face.

He has no desire,
To look for a friend,
For his heart is a stone,
What cruel things God sends.

But rise from the ashes,
To a world without hate,
You must go to the tower
And unlock the gate.

Angels will rise,
From the clouds in the skies,
You must understand,
The purpose of this land,
It is . . . the future.

Samantha Dolan (11)
Reigate School

IN THE FUTURE

In the future, I think there'll be . . .
Robots instead of people,
Aliens for pets.
More transport to different planets,
Like cars or jumbo jets.
Lots of different foods,
That have never been found
And new sorts of insects,
Crawling underground.
Computers that can communicate,
From future to past,
Or find out who's slow
And who was really fast.
Whatever happens in the millennium
Should not change the way you are,
Because things might be different
But just think of yourself as a golden star.

Kexy Barrington (12)
Reigate School

FUTURE STUFF

Intergalactic flying cars
Robot slaves holiday on Mars.

Marvellous dreams will be fulfilled,
Wonderful places we will build.

Will the planets join in line,
Squash together, all be mine?

Go to town, buy a shop!
Eat scrumptious food till you pop!

The future will bring lots of things,
I can't wait till people invent wings!

Dogs walking humans on a lead
The future will be very strange indeed.

Andrea Holmes (11)
Reigate School

MILLENNIUM

In the millennium there will be new people
Being born,
Even animals, such as tigers.
Lions and frogs.
Inventions will be made:
Talking cars and life on Mars,
On Christmas Day things will change.
Like Christmas trees that talk,
Telling jokes and playing Christmas games.
Houses build up,
Houses come down.
Young people in,
Old people out,
We all live our life like this,
Our life is to live,
So enjoy, enjoy the
Millennium.

Emma Raynor (13)
Reigate School

FACE OF FUTURE

Busy, noisy, working people running around littering,
Cluttering Earth.
Screaming children, chatting mums.
A cloud approaches the sky.
Shattering voices to a silence.
The voice was loud, the voice was proud,
Booming loudly, booming proudly.
'The future is grey, it will make you suffer.'
Colour drifted away.
Happiness drifted away, all colour drifted.
Smiles drifted, singing drifted, spirits drifted.
Black rain dripped through pipes
I saw my sad face in a grey puddle and
Thought, is this the face of future?
Happiness was gone.

Louise Clark (11)
Reigate School

FUTURE VOICES

Millions of people getting ready for New Year's Day,
Infants and adults get packing to fly away.
Laughter and celebration spreads around the world,
Lovers doing limbo and giving it a whirl.
Everyone thinks how time has flown by,
Not to mention when they first said *hi*.
Newbury have already planned a party,
Ireland thought it was very arty.
Uncles and aunts go Christmas shopping,
Many others just make cakes and put on the toppings.
It's the millennium 2000!

Lesley Coomber (12)
Reigate School

FUTURE VOICES - THE FUTURE CALLS

No! Please no!
The present pleads,
I didn't do it!
The now tells,
I didn't say another word.
You did, didn't you?
I couldn't say another word,
I don't believe you!

Bruises, cuts and grazes,
On the outside,
Deep wounds and digs
On the inside.
The now whispers
The future calls
The children of now
Are the future.

We have deep digs to mend
These will take years
We have small cuts to mend
These will only take days.
If we stop it now
Do you think it won't happen again?
If we don't stop it,
Do you think it will happen again?

Kirsty Lawrence (11)
Reigate School

ROBOTS

Bombs
Dynamite
What's happened to the world?
Everywhere I look there's war and poverty.
People dying and starving,
There's not enough jobs for humans.
Robots with dark gloomy voices have taken over the world.
I'm sure there won't be any humans soon.
What happened in the past?
They said the future would be great,
Flying cars,
Computer communication,
That seems so long ago,
The world is forever gloomy
Darkness has taken over the world.

Jemma Wheeler (13)
Reigate School

I AM THE FUTURE

F   uture is just the beginning, that's what I believe!
U   p and down the world spins around and around!
T   o the future we go, ahead of us all!
U   npacking all the future which is all dark and mean!
R   unning into the future as fast as we can!
E   nding the past. Into the future as it's only the beginning!

The future is here at last!

Deanne Myers (11)
Reigate School

FUTURE VOICES

Future music
As loud as war
Future voices
As good as sugar.
Adventure
As good as life
Adventure
As lasting as a firm.
People in the future
Like people being able to fly
People in the future
As wonderful as honey.
Inventions of the future
As crazy as bungee jumping
Inventions of the future
As hands, as hands
Millennium
As nice as chocolate
Millennium
As clear as glass
Robots
As funny as a clown
Robots
As human as humans.

Lee Morley (12)
Reigate School

Future Fantastic

The future's fantastic,
The future's wonderful,
The future has talking cars,
Inventions like living on Mars.

Millennium 2000 was a great hit!
Although my dad stood there like a candlestick.
Now we make peace with the aliens green
And now it's time to feel the steam.
Life on Mars is just so cool.
Our teachers are aliens, there just so tall.
I wonder what the year 2000 will be like?
Hmmm . . . I wonder.

Lisamarie Osborne (12)
Reigate School

One Step Ahead . . .

A veil of black eerie mist,
That swarms and infests everything,
Nothing can escape its darkness . . .
As you walk through the haze you see another figure . . .
He calls himself the future,
He is one step ahead,
He sounds the voices of a million people,
He is just down the path,
Just down the stairs,
Just around the corner,
Just through the door,
Just up there . . .
He is one step ahead.

James Taylor (12)
Reigate School

THE FUTURE

The future
It's dark and dull
The air is polluted
And the water diluted,
With a highly toxic filth.

When the nukes hit Earth,
The Earth fell off its axis,
It began to drift towards the sun,
To the doom of everyone
The earth was sure to explode.

Earth was drawing closer,
The heat was now intense,
The children were all crying,
But their parents still were lying
That the Earth, would not, be destroyed.

As the Earth passed through the gases
The planet began to burn up
The sun blared and people were toasted
As for the Earth, it was roasted,
No one did survive.

Sam Sari (13)
Reigate School

FUTURE VOICES

Knock, knock, knock!
'Who's that?'
'It's me, the future and I'm here to tell you what the
Future will be like, so come on, let's go.'
'Go where?'
'To the future, silly.'

'We'll have talking cars,
We'll live on Mars.
We'll go on new adventures,
We'll have sweety detectors.
We'll be taught by a monkey,
It will be funky
And animals will talk for example cats,
We'll also have to wear funny little hats.'

'That's what the future will be like.'

Jocelyn Hatton (12)
Reigate School

FUTURE VOICES

The future voices call to me
But with desperate cries or ecstatic glee?
Only we can mould that fate,
Can we mould it before it's too late?

People sleeping on the streets,
In 40 years will I still meet?
Will racism have gone away
Failing to cloud another day?

Will Mother Nature finally see
That we are not her enemy?
Mankind as a single piece,
The wars and violence finally cease.

The future voices speak wisely to me
But can they make countless others see
That harmony's the only way?
But everybody needs a say.

Katie Squire (13)
Reigate School

MY DREAM OF THE FUTURE

Life in space, that's my dream,
Don't you get what I mean?
All those rocks flying by,
If you think about it, it is quite high.
Just a few metres (wow) above my head
I thought it was going to knock me dead.
Rocketing through the solar system we go,
Rocking up and down, to and fro.
When I landed, I met a mate,
Then someone turned up I really hate.
Two hours later we were lost in space
I went to sit down but someone was in my place.
10 minutes later, we were back on task
All of a sudden I was floating in an aircraft.
In the future it would be cool,
Wearing weird clothes you would look like a fool.

Daniel Hill (12)
Reigate School

MUSIC DREAM

I love music, it's almost my life,
I will love to be a popstar,
I always have fantasies about singing live,
I will never mime, I'll be out of place,
Everyone will tell by the look on my face.
Fame will be a great thing,
It won't change me for the world.
I will sign autographs and write fan mail
Back to all my fans.
I will make videos to play on MTV and the Box.
I'll dance on the videos and tour the world,
To see different places and have concerts to
Try to put on a good show.
I will meet all different stars
And go on kids shows like
The Disney Channel and Nickelodeon.
I will go on Live and Kicking so fans
Can call in and ask questions.
That is my dream of the future and I'm
Hoping some day it will come true!

Melissa McSorley (12)
Reigate School

FUTURE VOICES

For trips down to the seaside,
To trips up into space,
I am a future voice and body,
Yet you cannot see my face.

Invention of computers,
To the Millennium Bug,
From the cloning of a sheep
To the cloning of a slug.

There are so many different changes
From way back when I was born,
But the future changes everything,
The millennium, a break from the norm!

Beth Smith (13)
Reigate School

A LESSON FROM THE FUTURE

What does the future hold for you?
What are you expecting?
What are you going to do?
Why do you keep on watching?
Watching the extinct become smaller and smaller,
Things like this cannot go on,
Humans losing animal trust,
Help them now not later on.
The ozone layer's losing weight,
Air pollution will be its fate.
New inventions are what we need,
To keep us moving at good speed.
Sort out diseases that can harm,
Before they damage food, crops and farms.
Not forgetting the human race,
Who will be put at their pace.
So what does the future hold for you?
Have you changed your opinions too?
Because you are the future,
And what you do counts,
If you don't care now, the future will not mount.

Charlotte Batten (13)
Reigate School

THE LAST WHITE RHINO

I stood there all alone,
Wondering where the others were?
Am I the only one?
Where have they gone?
I weep as I stand here.
No one to play with,
Nothing to eat,
Help somebody.
Come and free me.
In this cage I feel locked up,
All day long people look and stare
Am I the last white rhino?
Am I?
They take my picture,
Never letting me rest,
Am I the last white rhino?
Am I?

Kayleigh Hiley (12)
Reigate School

FUTURE VOICES

Barry the bully
Was a horrible boy,
He picked on poor Nigel
And took his toy.

The ghost of future
Appeared one night
At the bottom of Barry's bed
And gave him a fright.

He said what would happen
If he carried on this way,
The price of no friends,
He'd have to pay.

He saw Nigel the next day
And gave back his toy,
Now Barry the bully
Is a nice little boy.

Steven Wilson (11)
Reigate School

TELL ME MY FUTURE?

The lines on your hand,
Or the tarot card,
Will depict your future,
Be it easy or hard.

Pick a card,
Or rub my face,
The future for you,
Will come into place.

Nobody knows,
What the future will hold,
As our lives are mapped out,
For each to unfold.

We each carry on,
In our own separate ways,
But our lives are so different,
We change every day.

Carly Marshall (13)
Reigate School

WHAT WILL THE FUTURE BE LIKE?

In the future I may think
Whether you have to write in pen and ink.
Will you have to come into lessons at school?
Or will you just be the toilet ghoul?
When you go on holiday, will you go on a rocket plane?
Or will it all happen outside your window pane?
In the future will it be
All gobbledegook and wizardry?
We don't know what the future will be like?
Will there be no cars and all motorbikes?
Will the inventions be very good?
Will we have to write with bits of wood?
But whatever happens in the future,
Will all be inside our computer.

Alex Horton (12)
Reigate School

YEARS FROM NOW

Imagine robot teachers
They're never ever happy.
Imagine using laptops
Pen and paper will be history.
Imagine how quick lunch will be
Just swallow down a capsule.
Imagine going to lessons
Just hop on board a hoverboard.
Imagine all the school trips
Rocket trips to Mars.

Robert MacKrell (11)
Reigate School

A FUTURE VOICE

The telephone, ha!
It has seen better days.
E-mail's the way to go now
What happened in the old days?

The television, I wish!
No one uses it now.
Computers have taken over
TVs they just look foul!

Books, they aren't made anymore,
You can read them on the internet.
All the different authors
The kids they treat the computer like a pet!

Buses, no such thing,
Cars aren't around too!
People travel by air nowadays
And any age can drive too!

I miss the TV, the phone and the books,
I miss the way I used to stand and cook.

I dream of the future but I just cannot see,
Anything changing back to the way it used to be!

Emma Waller (13)
Reigate School

I Have A Dream . . .

I have a dream that animals will survive,
No captivity, no cruelty.
White rhinos will exist,
No poachers, no killers.

I have a dream that pollution will shrink,
No petrol, no smoking.
Ozone holes will soon repair,
No ice age, no heat rise.

I have a dream that people will understand the
meaning of life,
No murders, no crime.
Treatments will be made,
No cancer, no disease.

I have a dream that the 3rd world will recover,
No poverty, no poor.
People will survive,
No starvation, no thirst.

I have a dream . . .

Jack Kirsch (13)
Reigate School

A Journey To A New Dimension

The day is new
The planet is too,

My pet alien little Zak
The one I carry on my back,
He is brother to tiny Zed
Who I carry on my head.

Because I have a floating car
I'd travel round and round Mars.

I could eat chocolate bars,
Just because I live on Mars.

That is what I think it will be like in the future on Mars.

Rachael Boon (11)
Reigate School

2000 AND BEYOND

The city of Atlantis has been discovered,
It has also been amazingly recovered,
You can see it, it looks Greek with statues of beautiful people,
Colourful mosaics and hundreds of steeples.

The Bermuda triangle is a magnetic force,
Scientists have overcome it and pulled out the wreckage with a
simple source.

Gravity has been defied and all the people float,
Transport is above the ground and there is no such thing as a boat.
G M crops have been banned for making the healthy sick,
Liquid nitrogen is the latest car fuel, and it's really quick.

Rhinos, panda bears and Tasmanian devils and more are all extinct,
All over the world there are memorial statues that make you
stop and think.
The world is quite a peaceful place, there's been no World War Three.
This is a wonderful time to live in the year 2083.

Now is a time when all nations bond,
These are the years 2000 and beyond.

Katie Mulhearn (12)
Reigate School

FUTURE VOICES

Many years from now,
School will be different.
There would be a monorail
So you wouldn't be late for classes.
There would be no pens or paper,
Only PC computers.
There would be no reading books,
There would be CD ROMs.
The teachers would be robots,
Who are grumpy all the time.
This is what I think school would
Be like in the future,
I wonder if it will be like that.

Peter Beckett (11)
Reigate School

WHAT WILL HAPPEN IN THE FUTURE?

I know the Earth will be danger red
And all the animals will probably be dead,
If this is so,
Then I want you to know,
What we are doing to the world.

Grey pollution fills the skies,
Burning everybody's eyes,
Empty seas, no marine life there,
All the trees have gone, but where?

I want you to know
What we are doing to the world.

Deborah Saunders (12)
Reigate School

FUTURE SCHOOL

Our teachers are robots,
They're very, very grumpy.
Food is really delicious
And also free.
We have our own servants,
They help us with our homework.
We have mini cars,
They take us to our class.
We have CD books,
They go into our computers.
We get to wear our own clothes,
Which is better than wearing our school clothes.
We have our own robot teachers,
Which is fun.
We have friends,
Some from other countries.
Our classes are made out of iron,
Which makes our classes look very different.
We get to take a pet to school,
Which gives us good company.
We have our own desks,
Which gives us more room.
We have no homework,
Which means we can have more time playing out.
We get to go home for dinner,
Which is better than having it at school.
We get our own changing rooms,
Which is better than sharing.
We get our own lockers,
Which is better than paying for them,
That's what I call a groovy future school.

Sara Wicks (11)
Reigate School

YEARS FROM NOW

Years from now, cars will fly,
Planes will be on the road,
People will fly around on hoverboards,
Animals will live in houses and people
Would live outside,
Animals will talk and people will
Just make noises.
Animals would be in charge of
The world and people wouldn't.
There will be no police force,
Criminals will be let free,
In some places there will be no oxygen,
When people die they will be
Made into robots,
That's good because that will
All happen years from now.

Bradley Snape (12)
Reigate School

FUTURE VOICES

I hear a voice inside my head
While I'm dozing in my bed.
The voice I hear sounds like mine,
A sweeter voice and quite refined.

The voice I hear is talking now,
Asking me questions what, where and how?
When I reply I sound so mature,
Is it me? I'm not quite sure.

I have a feeling deep inside,
I'm not ashamed I cannot hide
The love I feel for that sweet voice,
It is my son, I have no choice.

I had a glimpse of my future tonight,
I spoke with my son and it felt just right.
My future is with a wife and son,
I know my life will be full of fun!

Tom Robinson (11)
Reigate School

JOURNEY TO THE FUTURE . . .

Get inside our time machine,
Come and see just what I mean.
In this world we are protected;
Until now the future was undetected.

Into the future we travel,
A whole new world for us to unravel.
Even though our knowledge has advanced,
Living on this planet we take many a chance.

Pollution in the air; war on the ground,
There must be another solution to be found.
New ideas . . . cloning and computers to name a few,
But still there are things we must remember too.

Forget the spaceships and nuclear war,
Deep down we all know what we are here for.
I hope you will hear my warning,
For our end is soon to be dawning!

Cleo Bigwood (11)
Reigate School

THE YEAR 2000

The world unfolds to another fate,
Like a fresh, modern feast set upon my plate.
Our healthy bodies will no longer be in view,
Replaced by idle minds powered by gadgets from Dr Who.
The after time has come to enliven our brains,
Teaching us to operate new instruments,
To relieve us of common life pains,
More sparkling projects flood our untrained lives,
A whole new generation of the able and wise,
Digital, fax, modems, they'll all in the past,
For here comes forward a more complex cast.
No more trains and buses,
No more colleges and schools,
For within our humble homes, we will have the tools.
Our hands will be lively and busy,
By the touch of a button, it will grant all,
2000 will be heaven, or so they say to fool.
A vacation to the moon will be my distinction this year,
For all this technology has in conclusion brought it near.
A solution has been made, that identifies us clear,
My age imprinted on myself, the truth will lie right here.
The 19th century is history, a subject we revise,
We learn of their simple, yet puzzling lives.
Gasping breaths of air through the bustling streets,
Dodging in and out of the swarms of bees,
The word millennium to me, is a cluster of fear,
Everything different makes us shed a tear,
But where would we be without a unique life?
In a pattern of boredom, full of anger and strife.

Rachel Keen (13)
Reigate School

THE FUTURE?

What will the future be like?
Will there be flying cars
Or will there be none?
Will there be rockets, aliens
Or go back to cavemen?
Will the population go up to ten billion
Or down to zero?
Will there be new inventions
Or will we stay like we are?
Will the babies look weird and change
Or will they stay like they are?
Will there be new ways to communicate
Or will it all stay the same?
Will the food be a luxury
Or will we be eating each other?
Will we be living in bigger house
Or will we be living on the streets?
Will we be living on Mars
Or still on Earth?
Will there be big black lots of smoke
Or will there be none?
What do you think the future will be like?

Christopher Randall (13)
Reigate School

WHY?

Death and pain creeps everywhere,
An empty landscape battles with despair,
Eerie blocks of concrete loom around every corner,
The polluted grey smoke hangs over my window,
It is civilisation so bare.
I had a dream of beauty and happiness,
Animals and plants thrived everywhere,
I wish I had an animal to love and to care for,
But animals are so rare,
Imagine crystal clear streams cascading
Down high mountains into lush green valleys
Creatures sharing the Earth in harmony with us.
These are pointless dreams rather than reality,
Greed and selfishness poisoned our earth,
Man drained the soil form its precious resources
We are left with this barren landscape
With no hope of happiness or escape.

Jessica Reynolds (11)
Reigate School

I HAVE A DREAM

I have a dream about the future,
That teachers would come to school
On a motorbike and in leathers.

Our books will be little laptops
And we will push a button so it pops up.
I dream that we have robots too,
To dress us for PE and that lunch
Was capsules and had vitamins in.

When we get to school, a screen
Comes down with subjects on and we
Pushed a couple of subjects that we wanted to do that day.

Roller coasters would pick us up and take us to each lesson.
I have a dream that teachers were animals and they communicated
by a voice box attached to their head.
I have a dream that we have a Walkman and the teachers would give
us a tape to study and that was my dream.

Matthew Neale-Picard (11)
Reigate School

FUTURE VOICES

When I meet the future I wonder what it would say,
It could say something I wouldn't understand.
It could say something like 'aliens and invading the planet.'
Imagine the aliens, what they would look like?
What would they say?
What would they do?
The question I would ask is why?
The future voices I would hear, would say
'To be supreme.'
The future could be something great.
It could be something disastrous.
The only people who will know are the people
Whose future it is.
I wonder what my future will be?
Do you look forward to your future?
I do!

Joe Lloyd Pack (13)
Reigate School

A Bright Future?

A bright future?
Not in my theory.
I imagine the world will be taken over
By maybe aliens or robots that used to be people,
But because they died their organs got replaced by a robot body
So they could live on.
There will be no trees,
And some people will be living on different planets
Because of us being taken over by aliens or robots,
The world will be a different place.
There will be no animals of any sort
Because the air will be too badly polluted.
We will all be tortured,
And we will be slaves
For the aliens and robots.
A bright future?

Linzi Holmes (13)
Reigate School

Futurama

The teachers are all aliens,
And don't eat at all
And their favourite habit is
Sitting in the hall,
Listening to poems and things like that,
And in the school is a black and white cat.

The kids have floating cars,
And float to their next lesson.
Some of the bullies crash into the younger kids
And the cars are very fast.

The teachers give us homework every hour.
Our subjects are alien, zombie
Clingon, human and maths
And that's life in two thousand years.

Colin Peters (11)
Reigate School

LITTLE GREEN MAN

A little green man took my hand,
By the hand to a far off land,
A far off land where trees can't grow,
Famous landmarks hidden away never on show,
Where skyscrapers soar beyond the eye,
And you can't walk around you have to fly,
A land way after the millennium and E-mails
Where computers are considered as slow as snails,
The little man said, 'Look how far we've come.'
But I replied, 'Look at the damage that's been done.'
People walked about like lifeless ghosts,
'We've taken over' the little man boasts.
The sky above stained with war and pollution,
The little man said, 'We're predicting a human revolution.'
Over the years animals have been thinly scattered,
An Earth now so ugly, its mirror shattered,
The little green man then took me back home,
To where the trees stand tall and we're free to roam,
To where visions of nature aren't stored in Earth's attic,
To where the warnings from future voices aren't heard above the traffic.

Amy Shipham (13)
Reigate School

FUTURE VOICES

I dream of futuristic people,
Electronic cars,
Robots taking control over the world,
More people, to talk to,
Population raising, higher, expanding,
Animals dying out,
Replacing aliens,
Bringing dinosaurs,
No violence, no more killing,
Next generation,
We are!
Babies will change,
Growing up to be something different,
Wider acceptance of children's views,
Computerising what you want your babies to be,
Keeping to one language,
No bullies, no crimes,
Bringing new things to our world,
No smoking or pollution,
People, dinosaurs, voices, shouting,
Will the world end?

Vicky Wicks (13)
Reigate School

FUTURE VOICES

A baby would be nice,
Or a nice college job,
Maybe I could have some pet mice,
Now that would be nice!

A nice new suit,
Or a neat little traders job,
Maybe I could have a pet newt,
Now that would be cute!

A lovely new Parker pen,
Or a policeman job,
Maybe I could have a pet hen,
Now that would be noisy then!

A brand new car,
Or a lollipop man job,
Maybe I could have a pet iguana,
Now that wouldn't go far!

Adam Wolfe (11)
Reigate School

FUTURE VOICES

One day you will live in a perfect world,
A world where nothing is real apart from man and the Earth.
The capitals of countries are made into paradises,
The small towns are left to rot.
Peace rules the world now,
War is locked up in a deep, damp cell.
You look into the sky to see nothing,
Nothing but flying cars and skyscrapers that reach the roof.
At night you see no stars, but instead the lights from the skyscrapers.
Soon man will fly up to the moon and will be smiling back
down on Earth.
Although life may be perfect, it is full of complication,
The complications of life get in the way.
The only thing for man to conquer is love,
The feeling that talks to you and guides you through life.
That is all, you must overcome the rest of life yourself.

Mark Setters (13)
Reigate School

FUTURISTIC GENERATIONS

I had a dream, a dream of the future,
The children are our lives,
The light of our lives,
With more people to talk to,
More of a life to live.

I had a dream, a dream of the future,
No sexism, no racism, no crime,
As there would be no need,
Where there would be one language,
And one currency.

I had a dream, a dream of the future,
Children will be listened to,
Their thoughts and feelings accounted for,
Unlike ours now,
They'll see beyond the horizons,
Venture for their dreams,
Their time is of no essence.

I had a dream, a dream of the future,
No animal will ever be extinct,
Twenty-six white rhinos now,
Two hundred and sixty white rhinos in the future,
I had a dream, a dream of the future,
But this is only a dream.

Louise Winyard (13)
Reigate School

WE ARE THE FUTURE

We are the future for years to come,
New wonders, achievers and expectations;
School, college and uni we have passed.
Older then, with political views,
We will be voting for the Prime Minister.

Then if we get wed and have a child or two,
Soon they'd be the future and its voice;
Expressing their opinions for the world.
The changing times and humanities,
To create a modern domain to live in.

New technology invades the Earth,
Scientific theories are coming to life;
Computers are more important now.
Some people are polluting the world's future,
While others prevent global warning.
We are the future!

Jerilyn Lowry (13)
Reigate School

MY VOICE

M y future voice talking to me now, giving advice.

Y ears and years into the future, wondering what's going to happen.

V oices of other people, telling the future.

O nly voice, listening to the dangers that are possible.

I   n the future, voices will be able to give present voices good advice.

C omputer voices giving information about the future.

E verlasting voice, my voice.

Stacey Moore (11)
Reigate School

I Wonder

I wonder what will happen in 10, 15 or even 50 years from now?
Will we be living on the moon or underwater?
Will there be no jobs left for people because machines have taken over?
Will there be schools?

I wonder if you can go to the moon for a holiday?
I wonder what will happen in 50, 70 or even 90 years from now?
Will we be living on a different planet?
A different world?
Will aliens be living on our planet?
Will we be their slaves and they our leaders?
Will all the poor countries become rich and lead a normal life?
Of course I can only wonder these things but one day these things
                                                    might come true.

Robert Kay (11)
Reigate School

Future Voices

I'm hearing voices in my head,
Shouting, whispering, fast and slow,
Some of pleasure, some of dread.

I'm hearing voices in my head,
Who could it be? Why is it so?
Telling me what I have lying ahead.

I'm hearing voices in my head,
Is it a ghost, friend or foe?
These voices say my future's read.

Samantha Mellows (11)
Reigate School

2050

The buildings are triangular,
The vehicles are rectangular,
This is a city in the rush hour.
The population is pedantic,
The city's fast and frantic,
This is a city in the rush hour.
Discoloured and warped skies hold dark and deadly secrets,
The government tell lies about UFOs and aliens.
The people are all in fear of the communist dictators
Who rule over the city with strict and ruthless laws.
Civilians are in fear due to nuclear weapons.
The army's on the brink of ferociously brutal wars.
The worker's faces are grey
Due to work and no play,
This is a city in the rush hour.
Everybody is the same,
Everybody is the same!
This is a city in the rush hour.

James Benefield (13)
Reigate School

FUTURE VOICES

Future voices chatting away,
Trying to give us all the advice they can,
Desperately trying to make themselves heard,
To stop us doing stupid things,
Trying to make us unfoolish,
To help us out,
Or to help them,
Trying still trying.

Stephen Thomas (11)
Reigate School

CIRCLE OF HATE

Future voices - will they be heard or will the world's
communication draw to a halt?
Will computers and the Internet create a barrier
between civilisations?
The world's colour will die down.
The world will be a shadow formed by pollution
and buildings.
The green, blue and yellow of the world's colour
will be replaced by black and grey.
Red blazing fires creep over the green grass.
Anger, wars and blood cause our world to be a
huge circle of hate.
Trees, animals and flowers, drowned out by
robots, violence and skyscrapers.
Future voices - will they be heard or will they be
deafened by the world's scream for freedom from
the anger and fear that we have caused?

Sascha Jackson (13)
Reigate School

FUTURE VOICES

People on the moon,
Aliens on the Earth,
An interesting contrast.
It could happen you know,
It won't be long until we'll be
saying, 'Just popping into space
for a pint of milk.'
And instead of saying words in Spanish
you will be saying words in Zogokum.

Ross Maclachlan (11)
Reigate School

WE ARE THE FUTURE

'We are the future.'
I jerked round quickly,
There standing was a creepy looking creature,
Covered in armour, staring at me with green,
Evil glowing eyes.
'What are you, who are you.'
There was no reply.
Whatever it was, it was the first of its kind.
Then, down below an ant waddled past,
Flashing its yellow and blue eyes.
I stood up, on a nearby rock,
Worried that the ground will shake or suck me down.
I looked up at the sky, expecting it to be blue,
Instead it was grey with purple patches.
I glared down at my arms and legs,
They had gone to a shade of red, probably maroon.
I stared back at the creature before me,
It stared back, made a weird howling sound,
And ran behind a tree.
What was going on?
I had just realised.
I was one of those things.
I was more concerned for my wife and kids than . . .

Would I ever change back to my normal self?
I'm no different to anyone else,
Why have I changed?
What does the future hold?

Jason Mellows (13)
Reigate School

THE FUTURE SPEAKS TO ME

The future speaks to me,
It tells me of the fears we may face,
War, poverty, deaths, crimes,
He asks me, 'Is that what you want?'
I answer, 'No.'
He tells me the problems we may come into,
Pollution; extinction; disease;
Countries at war;
Animals being killed, slaughtered,
Pain, fear, tears;
No cheers;
Single parents as a daily pattern;
Violence, aggression, salty showers of tears,
Around the modern home;
The future used to look bright,
But the problems
We still have to fight.

Laura O'Callaghan (13)
Reigate School

FUTURE VOICES

I once heard a voice,
A distant, far away voice,
A voice almost from the future,
A voice of things to come.

What will happen to me?
What is the future like?
So many questions,
With answers like:

What will I look like?
Have you visited a star?
Has anybody visited you
From near or far?

A familiar voice replies,
A reply I would myself have said,
'Wait and see I say,'
And the voice stopped dead.

Daniel Maxwell (12)
Reigate School

FUTURE VOICES

Heart talking from the future.
What do I follow heart or head?
Think of the future voices.

> Heart says go to college,
> My head says take a year out,
> Please someone help me decide.

Babies, children and elderly people
All need our help at some stage,
I hope I can help.

> The voice of the millennium.
> Every single person is excited to hear,
> Celebrate the birth of Jesus.

Wondering what road to follow.
Warnings saying no don't do that yet.
Advice from the future world.

Emma Howell (11)
Reigate School

FUTURE VOICES

A man from 14 Baker Street
felt a rumbling beneath his feet.
He jumped up high
as if to touch the sky
and his head went straight through the ceiling.
The hole grew wide
and he climbed inside.
He found himself in a big, blue room,
the room went dark,
he heard a bark,
and from nowhere came a humongous shark.
It led him to
a woman called Sue.
She looked very futuristic,
that drove the man totally ballistic.
Forever she was talking to him,
then she turned the lights down dim
and explained how in the future
he would be famous
and rule the world.
From that day on he still hears voices
telling him that he will be famous.
From that day on he still is waiting,
waiting for that special day.

Ian Phizackerley (11)
Reigate School

IN THE FUTURE

In the future I think it would be sad
because there will be a lot more poachers
and that will be bad.
There won't be any white rhinos
left and no Indian or African
elephants and as for the snakes
there won't be any, no rattlesnakes,
no pythons.
There won't be any Chinese pandas
or bears, I think they get killed for theft
(I mean for food).
The world will be full of domestic animals
even though they are so cute.
There will be dogs, cats, rabbits,
gerbils, hamsters and budgies.
Why oh why do the poachers
kill these lovely animals?
Is it for money?
Is it for fun?
Nobody knows!
In the future I think there
will be no more of those cheeky chimps
or big, strong gorillas or those lovely
sloths, the poachers do this,
They chop up their habitat.
In the future I think it would be sad
because there will be a lot more
poachers and that will be bad.
So please oh please stop
all your poaching.

Joe Wolfe (12)
Reigate School

FUTURE VOICES

Looking back on the past today,
Everything seems different;
Electronic teachers,
Flying cars,
And even life on Mars.
People talking,
People walking,
It all seems the same,
Well not;
People's voices screaming and screeching,
People driving around and flying around,
No one ever walks.
I wonder how life will be one thousand years from now.

Keely Woolsey (12)
Reigate School

WHAT'S THIS?

Ouch!
What's this? I'll open it and see.
The Sun,
The Times,
The Daily Mail,
A family tree?
The papers say 30th December 1999,
That was 15 years ago in time!

How about this family tree?
The Robinsons,
Hang on this is a time capsule.
I wonder if we could use this in history?

Siân Peters (11)
Reigate School

FUTURE VOICES

I heard a voice repeatedly spinning through my head,
Saying, 'Don't jump, don't jump!'
But I just said,
'I'll be all right, I'll only get a bump.'
'You might get more than that.'
'Perhaps I will, perhaps I won't.'
'What if you land on that cat?'
'It will run away so I won't.'
'I still advise you not to jump!'
'I don't care what you say, here I go.'
'I told you not to jump,
Now you've landed in the dump!'
'Oh no, I'm stuck and it's just started to snow.'
'Perhaps you were right,
I shouldn't have jumped.'

Lucy Taylor (11)
Reigate School

FUTURE VOICES

When I am older
I think people will have robots
to help you with your chores.

When I am older
I think people will be
living on the moon.

When I am older
I think computers
will talk to you.

Kathrynn Wood (12)
Reigate School

FUTURE VOICES

'Hi.'

'Who are you?'

'I'm you but I'm older and wiser than you.'

'You're me but . . .'

'I'm you in the future.'

'Oh . . .hi, what's it like in the future -
full of computers and very technical?'

'Yes, it's great, automatic cars, planes
and trains . . .'

'Wicked.'

'Wicked, that's old.'

'What do you mean that's old?'

'No one uses it anymore.'

'So what do you use?'

'Superfonic, cyberant, sconictant.'

'They won't be popular now.'

'Though more animals are extinct,
trees are rare, and flowers are artificial.'

'Oh . . . so how do you . . . well . . . breathe?'

'It's very confusing, there are sort of fans
which blow out oxygen, they're everywhere.'

'Oh . . . I think it sounds better in 1999 (the
present) than in the future.'

'Well see you cyberfriend.'

'Yes . . . bye . . . voice of the future.'

'See you in the future.'

Louise Newman (12)
Reigate School

FUTURE VOICES

Who do I hear in my head?
Why do I hear it in my head?
What does it mean?
'Be prepared' I hear in my head,
Maybe to be prepared for school.

I keep on hearing these voices,
Not my voices.
Is it God in my head?
Is it my dead grandad in my head?
Maybe I should be prepared for something important.

The voices stopped today,
The day I forgot my PE kit.
The voices maybe telling me to be prepared for PE.

Laura Smith (11)
Reigate School

FUTURE VOICES

Future voices coming now,
Future voices make you say wow.
But in the future they don't use that,
The word for *wow* is simply tat.
Words don't mean what they used to,
It took me some getting used to.
Every voice is how it sounds,
It may be soft, it may be loud.
Even the aliens are talking about 'em,
Future voices you can't live without them.
Future voices loud and clear,
They tell you what you want to hear.

Kris Chay (12)
Reigate School

FUTURE VOICES

I predict I'll be
walking on the moon,
communicating with creatures from space.

I predict I'll be
a famous popstar
singing with other groups and being on TOTP.

I predict I'll be
put in the record books
for breaking the land speed record in a car.

I predict I'll be
rich with a talking maid
and a house full of small toy gadgets.

I predict I'll be
President of the USA,
I could tell people when and what to do.

I predict I'll be
the oldest man in the world
and be able to get a certificate from the Queen.

I hope I'll be
able to live up to thirty
and have a big bank account so I can go to Barbados.

Karl Parker (12)
Reigate School

FUTURE VOICES

'Hello.'
'Hello, who are you?'
'I'm your future twin, silly!
I've come to tell you what it's like in the future!'
'What do you mean?'
'Well, for example, pets, because -
Cats can wear hats,
Dogs sit on mats
next to the funky cats!
Pigs can fly,
And owls can make milk pies
full of magic flies!
The sea no longer stands
on the pebbles and the sand,
Instead there are tall buildings and flying cars
that can travel from Earth to Mars
in one split second!'
'To Mars?'
'Yes to Mars, where we live!'
'How come.'
'Well because the funky planet Earth
has too many at birth,
Not forgetting the -
Cats wearing hats,
Dogs sitting on mats
next to the funky cats!
Flying pigs,
And cows can make milk pies,
Full of magic flies!
That's what now stands as the future!'

Chloë Osborne (12)
Reigate School

WHAT WILL THE FUTURE BE LIKE!

I wonder what the future will be like, do you?
We might have electronic skateboards,
We will shoot everywhere with no work at all.
At school we would have laptops,
No books at all.
Bikes we don't have to pedal,
Isn't that fun!
You could go anywhere without getting worn out!
Automatic showers,
How cool is that!
Hovering cars,
No more getting stuck in traffic.
The future will be groovy!

Grant Walder (11)
Reigate School

MY FUTURE IN DISNEYLAND , PARIS

Disneyland, Paris
Space Mountain roller-coasters
Round and round the loops
The best ride ever.
Next Pepsi Max ride
360 feet high.
Scared as a mouse chased by a cat.
Dropped like an arrow pointing down.
Indigo train ride, no loops.
Fast 90 miles per hour.
My face was going funny
Screamed my eyes out.

Jamie Baker (11)
Reigate School

FUTURE VOICES

The point in life?
I hear you ask.
There's not a question
That is so vast.
Communication
Has definitely changed.
I cannot give you
Advice that's arranged.

But what do you mean,
You're a voice from the future
Telling me different
From what I believe?

Vegetarians - will show us the way.
Harm to animals
Has since gone away.
Learn to love, not hate
All forms of life,
You'll get the most:
Disagree in strife.

But animals live
To be killed and die,
Enjoyment in sport,
Fox hunting ban! Why?

The future will teach
I cannot explain
I hope you'll learn
We'll all do the same
So enjoy your life - while you have it,
Before you go back into the planet.

Alison Jones (12)
Reigate School

FUTURE VOICES

We are the voices of the children from the future,
Calling to the children of the past.
Change your ways, your acts, your life,
Or this world will not last.
Please do not, like you already have,
Leave it to us to clear this mess.
Think of the world *we* have to live in,
Don't leave us in this sadness.
As we climb over broken houses,
We hear the people cry.
This is what war brought you to;
How you and I will die.
The layers of pollution in the air,
Brought with it a cough and a tear.
Only *you* can change this world,
Past children, we hope you can hear.

We are the voices of the children from the future, listen.

Robyn Smith (12)
Reigate School

FUTURE VOICES

Future voices talking,
Voices building in my head.

Warning me about a big decision,
An event soon to happen in my life.

Unusual future language,
Cannot fully understand.

Voices gradually fading,
Future message I didn't receive.

Forever the message will be unknown,
An oddity, but not to the future voices.

Hanna Caplin (11)
Reigate School

CONVERSATION WITH AN ALIEN

'Excuse me.'
'How may I help?'
'I'm speaking from 2009.'
'But it's only '99.'
'Well I'm from the future.'
'Still using a computer.'
'No way, that's old hat!'
'Oh imagine that.'
'No, I'm using my ray gun.'
'Wow that sounds like fun.'
'Yeah it's mega groovy.'
'Mega groovy, that's so old.'
'I don't care, it's the best saying around!'
'Do you still walk on the ground?'
'No I use space shoes.'
'I heard about them in the news,
It was on Alien Net.'
'Just make sure you don't forget.'
'If I do I'll fall down dead.'
'If you do die on your head.'

Katy Heffer (12)
Reigate School

FUTURE VOICES

I woke up one morning to very bright lights,
And when I opened my eyes, had a bit of a fright.
Thirty-six eyes all staring down,
From three different monsters all blue, pink and brown.
'Put him in the cage,' they said,
When I heard that, I was sure I'd soon be dead.
I sat down and tried to pinch myself awake,
When suddenly I heard a human voice say, 'Are you okay?'
'What year is it, and where am I?'
'Well you're on the planet Saturn and the year's two thousand
and nine.'
'Wow! I'm in the future, I gleamed,
'With aliens and teleporters and virtual ice-creams!'
'But the future is not all that great,
Now the world has blown up, we all have to live in space.'
'I bet you're hungry after your trip,' said a robotic voice,
'There's pizza, chips and quite a large choice.'
'A robot servant, cool! It can even walk and talk,
What else do you have here, picture phones and time warps?'
'Cool! Wow! What decade do you live in?'
We say new and modern things like dark and kickin'.'
I realised I was out of date and missed ten years of time,
When suddenly it all went black and I woke up in real life!'

Nancy Williams (12)
Reigate School

FUTURE VOICES

In my mind, I imagine
what future voices would say.
I imagine them warning somebody,
about their choice of way.
I listen to the silent words
that form inside my head.
Like lubber slubber for jelly and pel for lead.
As I listen, I imagine,
what, or who, the people are.
For they could be aliens,
or even glittering stars.
I wonder if that life would be
the answer to my fantasy,
The long-lived life I dreamed about,
With new inventions that weren't tried out.
There's bound to be something different,
but whether it's new or not,
people's voices will sound strange,
or even, possibly, not.
I wonder how things would be different,
or whether they'd be strange?
But the knowledge of the future,
is still to be gained.

Rosanna Westwell (12)
Reigate School

FUTURE VOICES

Into the future I can see . . .
The millennium is coming up,
Are things going to change?
'Yes' I think,
Voices,
Are people going to speak, are they not?
I must know how and what,
Are we going to sing or scream
I need to know even if you have to ring,
I need to know if we are going to speak posh or snobbish,
I need to know even if we speak rubbish,
Are we going to speak like robots,
Spitting and splutting.

I need to know.

Kerry Morley (13)
Reigate School

FUTURE VOICES

Okay listen to me,
Let me see,
Will there be more fish in the sea,
More birds in the sky,
More clouds up high,
I wonder why, oh why?

Will there be more grass on the ground,
Will more extinct bones be found,
More creatures on the land,
Will there be any more sand?

What will the future be like,
I wonder in my mind
Will I like it or will I not?
The future is coming.

Emma Ward (12)
Reigate School

FUTURE VOICES

I can hear voices,
Weird voices,
Voices that sound robotic,
Mechanical voices,
Words from the 70s,
'Groovy,' I hear them cry.
It's almost like a time warp,
It may just be in my mind,
But it sounds so real,
The sounds maybe from a faraway land,
Past the millennium voices,
'Hello' said the robot,
I don't know what to say,
Should I talk to them in Spanish,
Or in a mechanical voice?
I spoke back,
I spoke in 70's style,
A weird voice which I never use,
Shall I run away
Or shall I stay?

Tim Morris (12)
Reigate School

A FUTURE WORLD

A voice from the future is talking to me,
It is talking about new technology.
New inventions such as robots that do as you say,
They can do all your work while you sit and play.
What to expect in the next few years of my life,
What to expect about conflict or strife.

Cars will talk to us and tell us the way,
So we'll finish our journey without delay.

Houses will run off solar power alone,
They'll be so quiet, there won't be a drone.

The Earth will be safer the future is bright,
No poverty, sickness, the world will be right.

A voice from the future is telling me,
The world will be better, just wait and see.

Laura Catt (12)
Reigate School

FUTURE VOICES

A voice from the future is talking to me,
Is it a he or is it a she?
I think it's a she who's talking to me,
I wonder what she is saying.

What's it like in the past?
Does everyone eat fast?
So the old typewriter did not last!
Yesterday is now the past.

What's it like in the future?
Is everything still big and small?
Have dinosaurs come back from the dead,
And do people still sleep in a bed?

Do you still have computers,
So we can surf the net?
Do you still have cars
When we holiday on Mars?

Louise Dearmun (13)
Reigate School

FUTURE SCHOOL

Our teachers are all robots
It's great when they run out of batteries
But they are all miserable.

We have computers instead of books
You just say something
And it comes up without you doing anything.

We don't have boring dinner lines
We do not get served by scary dinner ladies
We have our own waiter.

To get to our classes
We have a neat little car.

We have a cool locker to carry
Instead of a bag.

That's my school of the future.

Adam King (11)
Reigate School

FUTURE VOICES

New technology is upon us,

           New computers can talk to us.

Soon there will be robots who can talk.

           Also the millennium is upon us.

Already we can hear the voice of the millennium,

           'I told you this would happen'

'Who's that?'

           'It's you ten years into the future.'

'Yeah, I thought this would happen, but not this quickly.'

           'Well it has and you get to use it all.'

Andrew Wyeth (11)
Reigate School

FUTURE VOICES

Just then I heard something,
Something weird and mysterious.
This was not tedious,
This was exciting.
I didn't know what to think,
I wasn't seeing I was hearing.
Hearing a voice, a child's voice,
The voice told me that,
I shouldn't marry Matt.

Matt who's Matt I thought,
'Matt is your future boyfriend,' said the voice.
'I am your future daughter,
If you marry Matt I won't be born,
He will make your heart torn.'
I never heard the voice again, until . . .
I had a daughter.

Jessica Twitchin (11)
Reigate School

FUTURE VOICES

In the future it does not smile, it frowns at us
We are waiting for the future, the future controls us.
There is no way we can tell what the future holds.
What the futures tells us, there is no way we can change it.
Maybe the future's fixed.
Maybe the future's running wild.
The future maybe big, tall buildings
Maybe we will have to wear special suits to protect us from the
violent sun's rays.
Maybe the future will become the past.
Maybe when we reach 2003, the clocks will tick back.
Do we really want to know the future?
Do we want to know when and how we die?
Won't that spoil the surprise of life?
Destroy your hopes of the future.
If the future has been written,
It doesn't matter what you do.
I want to decide my future.
I don't know about you.
The voices of the future could give us a clue.

Michael Breathwick (13)
Reigate School

VOICES OF THE MILLENNIUM

There are voices going round my head
Predicting my future.
People are screaming in my ear
'The world's going to end
The world's ending in the millennium.'
The voices in my head are driving me mad
Telling me that I'm going to have a miserable life.
'Listen to me, don't you care if the world's going to end?'
People keep screaming in my ear.

'Wake up it's time for school.'
'*Mum* I had a dream I know what's going to happen
The world's going to *end* in the millennium.'
'Of course it is!'

Patsy Jade McMenamin (11)
Reigate School

TRANSPORT OF THE FUTURE

In the future will there by flying cars or ground cars?
There maybe floating cars made for school.
Will trains have around 1003 mph?
Much faster than normal trains.
Will super cars exist?
We don't know.
There maybe a spacecraft built for space travel.
Lamborghini maybe the fastest car in the world.
Goody!

Ashley Braithwaite (11)
Reigate School

THE CAT

An angry Chinaman,
The fur reminds me of autumn.
At night she quickly but quietly scuttles
gently across the garden green.
Ears like baby leaves.
Hunger starts.
Her rage gets bigger, grabs a paw of food.
Chomps like a lion on rough bones,
Growling like angry dogs
Guarding important documents.
Paws like a plastic saucepan
From a doll's house
Sizzling on a plastic cooker.

Fizz-gig.

Shiona Maisey (12)
St Bede's School, Redhill

MOPPET THE CAT

She sneaks along the polished floor.
The steps creaked
As she slowly ambled upwards,
Her green eyes flashing in the dark.
Her brown and white fur glossy in the moonlight.

Her black and white feet squeaked the door.
Her tiny tongue lapped up the sparkling water
And downwards she went to the cold, locked door
She wished to get through.

Benedict Lloyd (12)
St Bede's School, Redhill

BULBS, GUINEA PIG OF THE WORLD

She snuggles into my dressing gown,
Diving deeper and deeper
Tickling my skin.
With little black eyes and a snub diamond nose.
Floppy ears like patches of rags sewn onto a small soft body.
She scuttles around chasing her sister,
Like a crab on a beach.
A dusty coat of fur, fine and smooth.
But dare you stroke her face
Where nasty little nippers lie beneath the
lips of pink flesh?

Louise Dungate (12)
St Bede's School, Redhill

LOVE

Mix in some roses and passion
Sprinkle a bit of honey and humour
Simmer for 10 minutes on moderate gossip
Melt some candy and chocolate
Mix together
Add some laughter
And sweetness and light.

Perfect.

Emma Thom (15)
St Peter's Catholic Comprehensive School, Guildford

RECIPE FOR HATE

Take a few ripe fists,
Lightly simmer.
Throw in a few choice curses,
Cook till smoking.
Put in some vicious stares,
Grill for an hour or so.
Pour in two bottles of blood,
Boil for half an hour.
Toss in a few malicious notes,
Fry and add some poison.
Whisk a few claps of thunder and some lightning,
Cook for two hours,
Serve warm.

Ruari Mostyn (12)
St Peter's Catholic Comprehensive School, Guildford

LAUGHTER

Take a Parisian *atmosphere*
Mix with 3 ounces of *good company*
Stir in some *humour*
Bake until *happy*

Garnish with a *celebration*
Add a pinch of *sunshine*
And serve at any *occasion.*

Tim Spruell (15)
St Peter's Catholic Comprehensive School, Guildford

THE STRANGER

See into the future,
See into the past,
I've got to tell you what
I see in the glass.
Tall, dark stranger
Knocking on your door,
Looking through your window,
What's he looking for?
Don't act crazy or
Close your eyes
Stand very still
Keep very quiet.

See into the mind,
See into the brain
Trying to reason
Why he's out again.
Slipping and sliding
Out of the shades
Don't even try hiding
He'll find you again.

Cold, cold steel
A whisper at night
He'll be at your side
With a smile
And a knife.
Don't try to run
You'd be a fool:
He's right beside you
Ever so cruel.

Stand very still
Your heart is beating
Just like a drum
He turns
His face
Towards you
And . . .

Moves on.

Paul Reeves (15)
St Peter's Catholic Comprehensive School, Guildford

A TURN OF THE LAMP

Life is what happens when you're making another plan,
And literature is a child's first word.
A gale is the blow from an indoor fan,
Freedom the flight of a bird.
Sorrow is nothing but a feeling,
Love is no more than a state.
Cuisine is milk congealing
And poetry just words on a page.

A smile is a murderous glance,
And cleanliness is purity of the soul.
You can swing but you may never dance,
You can spark without any coal.

Sometimes a turn of the lamp in the dead of the night,
Makes you see things in a different light.

Joni Clifford (16)
St Peter's Catholic Comprehensive School, Guildford

EXTREME

It's extreme, it's crazy,
It's insane:
I don't know why,
I love it.
It's the thrill, the excitement,
The heat you get.
It's extreme, it's crazy,
It's insane.
You can do what you want,
Whether it's jumping off cliffs
Or riding your bike.
It's a mixture of pleasure and pain.
Whatever you do,
Whatever you want;
It's extreme, it's crazy,
It's insane.

David Billam (13)
St Peter's Catholic Comprehensive School, Guildford

COSMIC MILLENNIUM

The year 2000!
Those magical words
Since last Christmas
It's all I've heard!

The bug, the parties
It's going to be great!
We can forget
All the bad things we hate.

We're living in a space age
As the modern generation
But sometimes I think
We're the worst since creation!

We leave the 1900s
To make a brand new start
But laziness will spoil it
So please just do your part!

Samantha Noonan (11)
St Peter's Catholic Comprehensive School, Guildford

HAPPINESS

Ingredients:

A couple of good friends,
A bit of laughter,
Some good weather,
A pinch of love,
A handful of fun,
An ounce of excitement,
And a tonne of energy.

Method:

Take a couple of good friends and mix slowly with a
handful of laughter.
Stir in some good weather and add a tonne of energy.
Mix a pinch of love and a pinch of excitement in and
leave till red (not too red otherwise it will turn into anger.)
Gently mix in a handful of fun.
Put in the oven at 100°C and leave till giggling hard.

Elizabeth Oliver (11)
St Peter's Catholic Comprehensive School, Guildford

IF I WERE . . .

If I were an animal,
I would be a cat,
So I could be free.

If I were a building,
I would be a flat,
So I could meet lots of new people.

If I were a colour,
I would be blue,
So I could rule the ocean and sky.

If I were water,
I would be the ocean,
So I could be big and deep.

If I were a fruit,
I would be an apple,
So I could be hard and crunchy.

If I were a word,
I would be *a*,
Because you can be anything you like.

Rowina Merritt (11)
St Peter's Catholic Comprehensive School, Guildford

MARY HAD A LITTLE MAN

Mary had a little man
His chest was silky smooth
And every time a hair grew there
That hair she did remove.

Alice White (16)
St Peter's Catholic Comprehensive School, Guildford

HATE

Ingredients:

2 - lightly poached tempers
4 - tightly clenched fists
500g - grated feelings
20 - deep fried rumours
2 - drops of essence of torment
1 - tin of darkest clouds
Some fury.

Whip the tempers until bubbling furiously.
Then stir in the fists.
Allow to rise for 40 minutes.

When hot, stir in the grated feelings,
And fold in the rumours.
Next, boil in the darkest clouds
Adding the essence of torment.

Leave to simmer for 30 minutes.

Sprinkle evenly with fury
And bake until

Hard.

Dominic Mattos (15)
St Peter's Catholic Comprehensive School, Guildford

FUTURE VOICES

Children's voices are
our future:
a future of love,
a future of care,
a future of joy and laughter,
a future of hatred,
a future of war.

Who knows?

We do.

Lisa Kelly (13)
St Peter's Catholic Comprehensive School, Guildford

THE CROOKED MAN GOES STRAIGHT

There was a tall, straight man,
And he went a tall straight mile.
He found a nice new sixpence,
Upon a nice new stile.
He bought a normal cat,
Which caught a normal mouse
And they all lived together,
In a normal,
Boring house.

Anne-Marie O'Reilly (15)
St Peter's Catholic Comprehensive School, Guildford

INTERGALACTIC FOOTBALL

Intergalactic football league
The battle of the Sun's cup final,
Green aliens fee is 1.5sh
A 50,000 crowd is expected from
Around the universe
To watch
Mars V Jupiter.

For the final game,
Mars beat Neptune, Pluto and Venus,
Jupiter beat Mercury, Saturn and Uranus.
Earth
Is the referee.

Mars win the toss and decide to kick
Away from the sun's rays.
Jupiter put the meteorite on the centre spot
and kick-off.
Mars comes in with a crunching tackle
and dribbles to the stars,
which marked the goal.

Now only a few seconds
left
until
Mars
wins.

Patrick Kinal (12)
St Peter's Catholic Comprehensive School, Guildford

MAYBE

Maybe boys could cook,
Maybe boys could fly,
Maybe boys could think ahead,
Maybe boys are aliens,
Maybe boys are really ants,
Maybe boys are geniuses,
Maybe boys will see sense one day,
Maybe boys will be slaves to girls,
Maybe boys have special powers,
Maybe boys have got a sense of humour,
Maybe boys have gone too far,
Maybe boys could behave,
Maybe boys are telepathic,
Maybe boys will grow into men,
Maybe boys have a cunning side.

Anything is possible.

Amanda Dickinson (12)
St Peter's Catholic Comprehensive School, Guildford

RED

Red is the colour of a clown's nose.
It is my heart over-flowing with love.
It is the lipstick on a beautiful woman.
It is the fire bell ringing loudly.
It is the red, glowing sun,
floating on the horizon at sunset.
It is a single red rose blooming on a bush,
waiting to be picked.

Joseph Watts (11)
St Peter's Catholic Comprehensive School, Guildford

IF I WERE . . .

If I were an animal
I'd be a hippo
So I could lie in thick, cold mud.

If I were a building
I'd be a house
For families to enjoy.

If I were a colour
I'd be green
The colour of a healthy world.

If I were water
I'd be the salty sea
So ships could lie on me.

If I were a fruit
I'd be a juicy apple
So people could quench their thirst on me.

If I were a word
I'd be a deadly poison
And devour all the people that drink me.

Nicholas Worsley (11)
St Peter's Catholic Comprehensive School, Guildford

IF I WERE . . .

If I were an animal,
I would be a puppy,
So I could lick people's arms and legs,
And bite off kittens' tails.

If I were a building,
I would be an evil hut,
To capture little children,
And gobble them all up.

If I were a colour,
I would be black and blue,
To inspire people,
And make them smile all through.

If I were water,
I would be a fountain,
To be admired,
And found beautiful.

If I were a fruit,
I would be an apple,
Nice and juicy to suck on,
Until you've gone all through.

If I were a word,
I would be a connective,
To join onto other words,
And make them even better.

Ewa Gorska (11)
St Peter's Catholic Comprehensive School, Guildford

EDUCATION

I walk into school
I look round: bars on the window
Trapping our freedom.
As soon as I walk in they control
What I feel,
What I think,
When I think it.
Chips in our minds make us feel like
We are in some sort of
prison.

But this technology tells us
We are smarter
than our ancestors.
We know our universe so well
that we can name
every star.
We dream of being the first man
On Pluto.

We dream.

Sophie Richards (12)
St Peter's Catholic Comprehensive School, Guildford

FUTURE VOICES

In the future I hear,
I hear trouble lurking,
The trouble is about children,
Children that are homeless,
Children who are poor,
I feel sorry for their poor little souls,
I hear shouting and arguing,
Children who are depressed,
Children who are fed up with their parents arguing
But no matter what happens to the children,
I would still love them all very much.
I hope that every child who is not as wealthy as other people
doesn't worry.
The children are to look forward to the future
And not make the same mistakes as their parents.
The children deserve love, peace and harmony.
The children should do what their hearts' desire.

Abby O'Dowd (12)
St Peter's Catholic Comprehensive School, Guildford

OR SO I'VE BEEN TOLD

Cars of the future
will be big and bold.
They will have flashy colours
Or so I've been told.

It will have a mind of its own
and control the road.
It will be like a house
Or so I've been told.

It will have strong wings
which will fold and unfold
with the push of a button
or so I've been told.

It will have a kitchen and bathroom
That I'll paint blue and gold.
The greatest car ever
Or so I've been told.

Beckie Harrison (12)
St Peter's Catholic Comprehensive School, Guildford

A FUTURE VOICE

A future voice is something,
something I do not know.
It's a thing that I just dream about,
think about,
speak about.
My friends all think I'm bonkers.
They say I'm going
mad.
I try to tell them
what I hear,
but they just say
'You're sad!'

Claire Ganderton (12)
St Peter's Catholic Comprehensive School, Guildford

MUSIC

Loud and furious, the music rumbles,
creating and affecting our different moods,
Telling us what to think and do,
and when we want to do it.
Different songs mean different moods;
Jazz and pop,
Romantic and blues.
Party and groovy, love and sadness, are just
a few of what's to come.
Virtual singers, but realistic dancers,
shouldn't it be the other way round?
Songs that hypnotise us and tell us
what to do, and what we are made to listen to.
Music which has become so competitive,
it is to die for and
Music which can control our minds
and form great armies of dumb zombies.
World domination which results in
microchips in tapes and stereos,
Is this really how music is going to turn out?

Genevieve Findlater (12)
St Peter's Catholic Comprehensive School, Guildford

FUTURE ANIMALS

Animals will have parties,
play poker or gin,
Dolphins will fly
and birds will swim.

Animals will have human pets,
they'll wear clothes and talk
and also, quite amazingly,
fish will learn how to walk.

They'll have their own television shows
they'll play sport and drive cars,
some will paint and some will draw
and others sing and dance.

They'll all be gymnasts,
visit humans in the zoo,
Some will style their new-grown hair
While others doze and snooze.

They'll talk, they'll walk,
Play sport and drive.
What a strange world this will be
When it finally arrives.

Charlotte Poulter (13)
St Peter's Catholic Comprehensive School, Guildford

OWEN

Owen is fast
Owen is skilful
Owen is fast and scores a lot
Owen scores brilliant goals for Liverpool
Owen has scored a hat-trick
Owen never misses a shot at goal
Owen's passes are accurate and
Owen is
       Brilliant.

Gary Cox
St Piers School, Lingfield

CLOUDS

Clouds
Are a patchwork blanket,
Where angels sit having a picnic.
Are they big balls of cotton wool or candyfloss?
Is someone hiding among the clouds?
Sometimes they get angry and cry,
Maybe they can see what we are
Doing to our world.

Amanda Rapley-Redfern
St Piers School, Lingfield

THE WIND'S WHISPER

The wind was rustling,
Whispering away:
The future, the future,
A brand new day.

'What will come?
What will be?'
It questioned,
As it ran around me.

'Will it bring peace?
Will it bring war?'
It wondered as it
Rapped on my door.

'New ways of life,
New things to do,'
It spoke, it whispered,
It wondered too.

A life, a new life,
Not so far away,
Enclosing, encroaching
Day by day.

The wind, it whispered
As it floated away
The future, the future,
A brand new way.

Kathryn Wright (13)
St Teresa's Senior School, Dorking

THE SUN IN THE PAST, PRESENT AND FUTURE

Up at dawn, and down at dusk,
This is my life, and my life to be,
I'm quite contented surrounded by blue,
I watch the Earth you see.

I watch them go about their jobs,
Oblivious to me,
They look at me and worship me,
They think I'm God, you see.

Now, everything has changed,
I'm just there to light their day,
I shine for them, I'm taken for granted,
I'm just some yellow ball,
That's been placed or planted.

They fire things up at me,
Silver, red and white,
Flashing and burning,
They know where they're going.
They take flight after flight.

I'll rise and descend,
For many more years,
And they'll fire new things,
Right past my ears.

I've seen the past where
They worshipped me,
And I've seen the present,
I'm just the sun you see.

I know the future,
It is an evil thing,
I will burn up,
I'll be just like them.

I'll descend but never come up.

Rebecca Kirby (14)
St Teresa's Senior School, Dorking

FUTURE WORLD

It is amazing how
I can't speak to my parents,
the things I want to say,
the things I would like to tell them.

Once I am older I can explain,
but I will probably forget by then.
Just think about the technology,
how advanced it will be
but by then my parents will be long gone

But probably somewhere in the world
Someone will save them from deadly diseases.

Maybe one day all the important people will go
and anyone can take over the world
and try to save us from extinction.

The world will die out one day and disappear,
Someone has to stop it.

Elizabeth Walton (14)
St Teresa's Senior School, Dorking

ALONE

I curl up in my bed
Unaware of the world around me.
I call for an answer
But there is no reply.
I am alone!
Bewildered!
Yet unknown to the land.
The future is in my hands.
A shiver runs through my spine.
Confidence is winning my battle.
I hear a voice,
Shivering and cold.
I say 'Listen.'
I lie back,
Let my mind take over.
I am the last of my kind!

Sophie Grant (13)
St Teresa's Senior School, Dorking

ALIEN VOICES

Gazing down at the spinning ball,
The little green men remembered the lost
Millennium
In the year 2000.

Much had changed since then,
The green men thought -
Of all the celebrations and joy,
But it had ended so suddenly.

The voices of aliens,
Had been heard everywhere.
Calling to them, shouting at them.
They had changed their lives for ever.

After all,
Their planet in the last millennium
Was called Earth.

Joanna Robinson (13)
St Teresa's Senior School, Dorking

LOST FOREVER

Bang! Gone!
Fallen! Lost!
Never to be seen again
As its usual form.

I stand here
With no one around
Like a silhouette
But not for long.

We live no longer
But humans will see us again
As a book, or paper
Even a pencil.

From woods to vans
Then factories to shops
Then home with *you*
Then dead again.

Christiana Wightman (13)
St Teresa's Senior School, Dorking

GOODBYE

Help!
I'm here, what am I to do?
Every hour, every second, every minute of the day
I'm creeping around
keeping my eyes peeled
my ears pricked to listen for the slightest movement.
My life is becoming miserable
I can't leap and bound over the countryside
For fear of my life.
Hunters leap from nowhere
Before you find your legs
They hold a gun to your body
Aim
Fire
Bang!
One more member of my family gone
Gone, gone, gone
Never to come back.

Catherine Sinnamon (13)
St Teresa's Senior School, Dorking

A DINOSAUR'S STORY

Who would think me a dinosaur, so grand
a creature of power and valour,
would sit upon a lonely prehistoric museum stand?

Once I roamed free upon vast desert sands
in search of war and triumph.
Now I am doomed to collect dust and be
touched by grubby little hands.

I am in my prime I can knock an animal
down with one hit!
My impressive torso full of life and prowess
but all I result in is a giant skeletal exhibit!

Emma Rumble (13)
St Teresa's Senior School, Dorking

FUTURE VOICES

You may not see the future,
Think of your children's children suff'ring.
They'll reach with outstretched arms.
It is to you they are calling.

Pollution all around them,
A teardrop from each eye
If we don't stop pollution
Our children's children die.

Think about the future,
'Tis not your head on the block!
We have to save the future,
Put to all evil, a stop.

It is not you who suffers
But the future is your choice
For in ev'ry heart that's pumping
There's a soul, a mind, a voice.

So as the century's dawning
And our souls have sunlight kissed,
You will hear them softly calling.
Future voices in the mist.

Samantha Dixon (13)
St Teresa's Senior School, Dorking

FOUL OR FAIR?

Time will not stay
Time will always go
Some times are happy
Some are full of woe.

As old times die
So new time is born
We should be glad of the new
Not just for some
But for all, me and you.

How do we know what to expect
When there is no way for us to check?

What do you think the future will hold
For me and for you, the young and the old?

How can we know how to prepare?
The future's unknown, will it be foul or fair?

Bronwyn Elliott (12)
St Teresa's Senior School, Dorking

THE LAST

I wish I had been killed with them,
I don't want to be left alone.
As I sit by my window,
watching the streets,
hoping someone will walk by.
I know they won't, they never will.
It is so quiet, you could hear a pin drop.
There is no sound, the world is dead.

As I curl up in my bed,
Crying myself to sleep.
I hope I wake up,
And this will be a dream.
I can't live without family and friends.
I'm the last one left of my kind.

Alana Cooper (13)
St Teresa's Senior School, Dorking

PAST VOICES

The voices of the past millennium slowly drift away,
Drowned out by our midnight celebrations,
in the hallway past the stairs.
The grandfather clock strikes twelve,
everyone gathers around.
To listen to his melodic music.

But the grandfather clock
has lived through the past
And has seen enough hatred
to fill his wooden heart.

He has lived through the war,
and the sound of the bombs seem so near
Just as though they are still here.
He has seen the Victorian families crowd into the hall
and generations grow from big to small.

But now his time has come to go,
And his wooden heart is starting to slow.
Just as he shuts his metal eyes,
He hears a distant baby cry,
The sound of a new life.

Nicola Shears (13)
St Teresa's Senior School, Dorking

THE MOUNTAIN

We are all sinking, drowning slowly,
Into the deep lake of the past.
Mothers, grans and children
tear away their hearts
for what was and how we used to be,
but we must go on and fight
the terrible worries before us.
They're bound to sting and bite.
It's a wound that will never heal
A crack that will never mend
But we must go on this journey
With all its twists and bends.

It now is coming quickly
The mountain we have to climb
Up and up we'll have to go
against the wall of time
to remind us of the past
The life that we once lived
but the slate is wiped clean.

Goodbye to two thousand
for now I must start to climb
my mountain.

Georgina Bottomley (13)
St Teresa's Senior School, Dorking

FUTURE VOICES

The mists of time have changed everything,
The entire voice of humans has vanished.
We are no longer the hunted,
The humans are now our prey.
My great, great grandfather speaks
Of humans hounding us for fun and sport
But now we chase them for just the same reason.

Unkind? Vicious? Harsh?
No, not at all.
If you think about it,
It's our revenge and a punishment
For what they did to us.

And when I think,
That everything is different,
I ask myself -
Was it for a specific reason?
But the pack and I
Feel it's their turn to suffer,
To plead for forgiveness.

Oh, yes, we make it fair,
Only two to four wolves per pack,
So that the humans have a reasonable chance.

We have a human,
In a very tiny cage,
Starving to death.
But our young ones wait at the door,
Ready to shred the past to bits.

Zoe Bygraves (13)
St Teresa's Senior School, Dorking

FUTURE VOICE

Here I am,
All alone,
The world is still,
All life is gone,
But my life is not.

Why am I here?
Why me to stay here,
All alone in this big, big world?

I remember when I used to
laugh and play,
all day,
until the sun set as beautiful
as the world it's in.

All I want now is to
touch the skin,
Of someone,
Something.
I just want to feel the
blood running beneath the skin,
of someone,
something,
Like rivers through mountains.
I want to run my hand
through the hairs on the skin,
Soft as silk,
I want someone to stare at me,
Long and hard,
I want them to keep
starring until I can see,
Clear as pools,
The crystals in their eyes.

I want someone to hold me,
Grasp me,
And stop me from falling,
But no,
I shall fall and graze my knee,
And I shall never see,
Those eyes, clear as pools.

If you had all just listened
when you were told,
I could touch that hair,
Soft as silk,
Feel that blood,
Smooth as rivers,
And most of all,
I would not be alone,
In this big, big world.

Rebecca Marshall (13)
St Teresa's Senior School, Dorking

MAN IS LIKE A SNAKE

Man is like a snake meandering through a vast and empty desert,
The hot, steaming sun beats down on his back,
Just as disaster beats down on ours.
The snake feels hunger, eating away at him,
Just as anger eats away at us.
The snake finds the sand difficult to grip on to
Just as we find true friends difficult to grasp and hold on to
But soon the snake will come to the end of his desert,
Just as we will come to the end of ours.

Elizabeth Trevor (11)
St Teresa's Senior School, Dorking

An Example

My father said
We can learn from Man.
Sometimes we can learn what not to do.
So I have made a study,
Of bones, books and past inventions.
Some of them are quite amusing.
What was left?
I was lost in imagination,
Then horror,
And finally a kind of contempt
For what I saw.
The earlier ones got it right,
Relying on their own thoughts and feelings,
Their own observations,
And the way they observed.
Not mistrust, weaponry and the opinions
Of others.
Not mechanics, technology,
And a community with as much
Force and power as
The voice of an ant,
Over a morally devoid
Political system.
One of their weapons
Nu-clee-ar
I think it's called
Had power.
It controlled Man,
Almost programmed them
To believe that it could solve all their problems.
It was a small voice in their heads.

It said:
'Everything that you despise,
I can remove.
Everything you think is wrong,
I can put right.'
It destroyed them
In the end.
There were many who believed,
It was wrong from the beginning.
They didn't matter.
They alone were not powerful enough.
For the good of society as a whole,
The important ones said.
You could see the explosion,
Light years away.
A scorching white light
That flowed in a steady stream.
Man.
What an example.

Natasha Kuler-Von-Der-Luhe (13)
St Teresa's Senior School, Dorking

FUTURE VOICES

'What is the time that we call 2000?' asked God
'The time that measures your son's visit to Earth,' replied Time.
'Did He bring peace?'
'Well it helped, but remember it takes time.'
'At least it brought love.'
'I have not to lie, again it brought some love, but not much.'
'Let's hope that 2000 will change it all.'
'To me 2000 is only a stepping stone that I know and can't tell.'

Lucy Parish (11)
St Teresa's Senior School, Dorking

THE FUTURE VOICE

I am frightened, my eyes closed and tightened,
Mother cried, I comforted her, she left and sighed
She came and she told me the news
I do not believe it, for it is just their views.

They think the world will come to an end,
To death straight away we all shall send,
We who live shall no longer be,
For we shall perish, so you see.

I shall ignore this future voice,
For it is all my own choice,
To believe or not to believe,
For the truth one day, we shall receive.

My life will change for better or worse,
Whichever one, there's no remorse.
Am I to die or am I to live?
This question drifts past me like a sieve.

At last, it will come to an end,
This question that drove me round the bend,
Will this future voice be right?
It shall blow us all out of sight.

Ada Dan-Anyiam (13)
St Teresa's Senior School, Dorking

A START OF A NEW WORLD

Come, come, don't be afraid,
Your time has come, let's fly away.
What I hear and what I see,
Angels talking and looking at me.
They say they want to show me my future,
About my sweetest and greatest granddaughter.

She was to marry a long time ago,
When Dave asked her to marry him she said no.
It scared me to think.
At first I did not accept it.
I know she did it for the future
It's going to be hectic.
She's as soft as a baby's bottom,
She will never be forgotten.
She has grown to be wise,
She is up for any surprise.
She'll rule the Earth as once I did,
Faster than an arrow shot by Cupid.

As now it is time to say our goodbyes,
She does not know, I will never open my eyes
As I'll be watching her up above
So I don't catch that darned Millennium Bug
Even if she has no children, let's still rejoice,
About all the other children
And their futuristic voice.

Aisha Ibrahim (13)
St Teresa's Senior School, Dorking

WILL THE FUTURE BE BRIGHT?

In the past we look to see how we evolved,
In the future we will look at how we will be,
We imagine the future as bright,
With robots and space stations,
We don't imagine dark,
Space, loneliness and poverty
Not poverty in the sense of money,
But in the sense of no feelings,
No love, no heart.
We think we treat each other and other races as equals
but in the future we might realise we didn't.
We persecute animals but after all we are animals,
so shouldn't we be persecuted as well?
We as people do wrong,
Since the beginning of human time
we have made species extinct,
in mind, in soul and body,
but which would come first?
We, ourselves, might be tortured.
Our children, our children's children
for centuries to come,
might think they too were living the right way,
Maybe it will be our own stupidity that wipes us out,
But if we're lucky, it will be a natural disaster,
Whatever happens to our race,
I hope it will come before the loss of heart.
You need to educate our children,
Not to read or write (even though these are important,)
but to teach them to love and trust,
These and these things only will save our world.

Isadora Martin-Dye (13)
St Teresa's Senior School, Dorking

WHAT HAS THE WORLD COME TO?

The robots have taken over,
We're the servants now,
We answer to their demands.
They treat us like a pile of dirt.
As they're the sun and we're the earth.

They have luxurious homes,
While we have a dirty old cupboard,
They have the most modern technology,
I have a ten year old toothbrush.

I hear voices in my head,
'You've been kidnapped,
The world never used to be like this.
Run away, set yourself free,'
Then I go back to reality.

We bend over backwards,
For the robots, who can't
Bend over at all.
If I am lucky I will get
A tablet of micro-food,
But I am not giving up hope.

I hate the future,
Stay in the past,
You don't know what
You have
Till you come here.

Lucy Hollingdale (13)
St Teresa's Senior School, Dorking

REVENGEFUL EARTH

The gruff growl of an old man
grumbling of cold and prices and bills.
The disgruntled moan of a businessman
as his electric bills rise again.

The worried sigh of a mother
as the air gets denser and denser.
The wearisome chant of an all-knowing crowd
protesting the release of the world.

The alarmed gasp of a college student,
reading the records of cancer.
The painful groan of a wounded soldier
who fought in words for food and land.

The fearful shriek of a drowning child
as water floods her home.
The pitiful weeping of a dying babe
as starvation grips her world.

The world rebels against its master,
who's tortured and poisoned it so;
the hate from wounds that man has inflicted,
has taken its toll at last.

Victoria Spalding (13)
St Teresa's Senior School, Dorking

FUTURE VOICES

I am amazed at the way that I think about the future.
Although I have to concentrate really hard,
To think about what will appear before my eyes.

Will it be the most hi-tec digital technology
Where everything is done for you?
How cool would that be?

But how does this happen?
I'm a human being, not an alien.
Why? How can I do such miracles?

I love the world the way it is
And why should all people want
To change the world in the future?

Am I really the future voice,
Who can describe what is to happen
In the future?

Please help me!

Emma Jones (13)
St Teresa's Senior School, Dorking

FUTURE VOICES

Oliver can't talk yet
I wonder what his first word will be!
Will it be Mummy or will it be Daddy?
Or will it be something completely different like
Computer? Nobody knows!
I wonder what Oliver's first job will be
Will he take after his dad and be a candlestick maker?
Or will he take after his mum and be a doctor?
Nobody knows!
All of this is in the future to us
And we really don't mind
What his first word or
His first job will be
Because this is in the future.

Claire Parker-Greene (13)
St Teresa's Senior School, Dorking

THE HOTEL

This is a place I will never forget,
You arrive to a warm welcome and leave with regret.
Your heart fills with joy, each day, every night,
Everyone inside is happy and bright.
When the time comes to go you will feel lonely and sad.
If you never come back I swear you'll go mad.
People forget all their troubles and woes,
For this is the place where happiness grows.
As you journey back home, you will never forget,
How you arrived to a warm welcome and left with regret.

Leony Shakespeare (13)
The Beacon School

TRAPPED

My dull unseeing eyes,
Staring through the unforgiving bars,
With nothing new to see.
I hear the muffled thunder of the crowds,
The harsh sounds of footsteps echo in my ears.
I open my mouth in a soundless cry.
With no ears to care, to hear me.
The bitter taste of the smog-filled air
Touched my taste buds.
I take in a deep breath,
And the smell of stale droppings hits me.
I feel tired.
I sit,
All alone,
And in a ball of misery
I fall asleep,
My last sense,
The touch of the cold, smooth cage floor.

Jenny Ellinor (13)
The Beacon School

BEE HAPPY

Bees are buzzing everywhere,
Bee happy, bee happy.
If you're lucky they will make you honey,
Bee happy, bee happy.

In winter they go bye, bye,
Bee happy, bee happy.
If they buzz run very fast,
Bee frightened, bee frightened!

Alex Bellamy (11)
The Beacon School

SADNESS

I feel a little sad,
And tell myself, 'Cheer up!'
I try to smile but can't,
My insides are yelling, 'Cry, cry.'
I try to stop myself,
I feel myself going red,
My eyes are watery.
Soon I can't stop myself,
I'm sobbing softly now
But it gets harder and harder,
Soon I am crying so hard my eyes hurt,
With tears streaming down my face,
I eventually manage to heal my cries,
Although I feel a little better,
My nose is pale pink,
And cheeks rosy red,
I go to the sink submerging my face in water,
I slowly pat my face dry,
And ponder why I started.

Andrea Kashani (12)
The Beacon School

I LIKE CAKE

I like cake.
I like garlic bread.
I like everything we can bake
To eat in my bed.

I like lollies.
I like chips.
I like eating lollies
With sherbet dips.

Kim Wyatt, Georgina Green & George Ayres (11)
The Park School

DRACULA

Dracula is a funny man
He has wings like a bat.
He sleeps in the toilet pan
And sings like a cat.

He sings at night with his guitar
And wakes everyone up.
He thinks he's a rock star
And drinks millions of pints of blood.

He sucks blood like bubblegum
Speaks like a fish.
He's got a hairy bum
And goofy teeth you wouldn't kiss.

He's got white cheeks, like a clown
Sick makeup and gungy hair,
Black and evil eyes that frown,
And keeps a monster bear.

He sounds mental and wears black shiny shoes,
He's itchy, scritchy full of fleas.
He lives in a bouncy castle, that's news!
Skinny, bony legs and knobbly knees.

Robert Daniels (12)
The Park School

MICKEY

My cat is black and white
My cat gives me a fright
In the middle of the night
He turns on the light

He plays with a mouse
In the house
He scampers on the path
He licks himself to have a bath.

He miaows to come in
My cat is not thin

He sleeps on the chair and leaves hair everywhere.

James Allington (11)
The Park School

MY GOLDFISH

My fish moves like a shark under the water.
My goldfish has two gills
He is orange.
He swims around in a pond.
He has two fins and one tail.
He eats fish food.
He blows bubbles under the water.
On top of the water there are lily pads and plants in the pond.
He swims like a dolphin but doesn't jump out.
He wiggles and wriggles in-between the plants.
He is a big gold fish.

Lizzie Graham (11)
The Park School

MY BLACK RABBIT

My rabbit is called Pat.
She is getting fat.
She eats too much.
She sleeps in her hutch.

She sits on Dad's knees
But she does not make Dad sneeze.
Pick her up and she growls.
In her run she prowls.

She nibbles nuts in her hutch
But tomatoes she will not touch.

Jack Pollard (11)
The Park School

I LIKE CHICKEN

I like chicken
I like my Sunday roast
I like finger licking
The very, very most.

I like sweets to eat
I like big fat sausages
I like lots of meat
And nice juicy oranges.

Dean East (11)
The Park School

TORNADO

It is a grey stormy sky
As little children start to cry
At the sound of winds so strong
As everything flies along
We know something has gone wrong.

Power lines sparking and lashing
Slates flying off roofs, go crashing
The tornado is twisting and turning
The cars flip over and are burning.

Frightened and scared underground,
People can hear a loud sound,
Of things flying around. I'm sad
This tornado is very bad.

Suddenly the wind calms down
And everything falls to the ground
Everyone is quiet and still
Everybody safe, but feeling ill.

It's all over.

Jason Griggs (11)
The Park School

MEN IN THE KITCHEN

Dinner is what's on the table,
When they arrive home.
Kebab on the last train,
Although I shouldn't moan:
If 'gourmet meal' is cooked,
Oh won't the whole world know!
But microwave box and lettuce leaf
Is all they have to show.

The kitchen is a chilling chamber
For males of the species.
Electric wires come alive,
Piercing swords cut finger pieces.
Burning safe where bodies melt,
The risk of torture is high.
It's rare to find a man who cooks,
Or even one to try!

Natasha Gifford (16)
Therfield School

THE KITCHEN OF PLEASURE

The soothing, yellow walls shine in the sun,
The sweet aroma of rising bread diffuses through the air
As Mum reaches for her morning coffee,
And Dad browses through the news,
Not a single word anywhere.

After school when I arrive home from a hectic day,
I slump into a chair and relax with a snack,
Looking out at the tranquil garden,
The birds playing in the trees and singing,
I make the most of it, before my brother gets back!

The setting sun paints the patio outside,
The television blasts out in the living room next door,
But the kitchen remains calm.
A hot chocolate in peace before I retire upstairs,
I hesitate on leaving, just five minutes more!

Among the soothing, yellow walls that glow with the moon,
The peaceful nature of daytime will arrive again soon.

Rachel Weston (16)
Therfield School

AUTUMN GARDEN

Autumn sunbeams penetrate the hazy cloud,
glistening upon the motionless pond,
dandelion heads spin effortlessly,
whirling and twirling in the midday air,
golden, crisp leaves of the maple graciously fall,
as if to savour any last moments of life,
busy lizzies with soft pink centres,
watch intently autumn leaves fall with fascination,
Towering fir trees defend the flowerbeds,
As though an army of a thousand men.
Gradually the sun disappears behind the cloud,
Shading the ants' nest pausing any movement,
It returns and the ants climb up the tall blades of grass,
Like nothing had happened.

Nicola Fenner (16)
Therfield School

THE HOLLY TREE

The holly tree sways in the cool, sharp breeze,
Its round, red berries give a bright, warm glow.
The snow under trees is cold and wet,
The great, grey sky gives a drizzly effect,
While the people in the house are warm and snug,
Sitting round the fire reading fairytale books,
The night grows near as they go to bed,
The forest outside gets dark and dreary,
But the holly tree still sways in the cool, sharp breeze.

Sophie Robb (12)
Tormead School

RAMESES' REVENGE

I'm in the queue.
I've been waiting for ages,
There's hardly any people in front of me,
It could be my turn next.
I can see the ride swinging up and over,
It's upside down! It's going round again!
Nervously I clutch at my mum's hand.
She's coming too. She's not scared.
At least, she doesn't show it if she is.
I can see the people on the ride getting off.
Can I get on this time?
Yes! The man is beckoning me to come through!
I'm walking down the path,
My mum is helping me into my seat. She's sitting down beside me!
Now I'm scared.
What's this? It's starting up! Help! Let me off!
I start to go up . . . and down.
Oh no! It looked terrible when . . . aaaaaaaah,
Up and down. Up and down.
I was in the queue . . . wooooah!
Up . . . and over!
And it is terrible! Help!
Here comes the water! I'm moving slowly towards it!
Help! I'm getting soaked! I can't breathe! Help . . .
And then, with a whoosh, I'm let down.
The water stops, so does the ride.
It was terrible, I think as I climb out.
Awful, horrible, the worst ride I've ever been on . . .
Mum? Can we go again?

Victoria Sparks (11)
Tormead School

WHAT WOULD WE DO WITHOUT?

What would we do without lights?
Would we use candles all the time?
What would we do without bricks?
Would we just lag wood together and get cold?

What would we do without electricity?
Would we just use coal?
What would we do without windows?
Would it be dark inside?

What would we do without education?
Would we just stay at home?
What would we do without heating?
Would we freeze to death?

What would we do without others?
What would we do without friends?
What would we do without family?
And what would the world do without me?

Rebecca Couzens (12)
Tormead School

TROUBLE

I have been asked to see the teacher,
Whatever shall I say?
I know it will be a disaster,
I will never live again.

Was my homework too untidy?
I will use an ink pen.
Was the writing a little windy?
I will never live again.

To the staffroom is where I went,
Preparing for my doom,
Perhaps she has called my parents.
I will never live again.

Holly Brooker (12)
Tormead School

MY DOG BILLY

I have a dog called Billy,
You have never met a dog more silly.
He is a bit of a fleabag though,
But I still love my Billy.

He is fat and spotty,
And very, very dotty,
He does moan a lot though,
But I still love my Billy.

Billy is my special dog,
He is much better than a fat mog.
He does have his nasty habits though,
But I still love my Billy.

Billy cannot run very fast,
In a race he would definitely come last.
He does leave muddy footprints everywhere though,
But I still love my Billy.

Billy got too much to handle,
His favourite game was 'hide the candle',
In the end we had to sell him, shame really,
But I will always love my Billy.

Eleanor Ewart (12)
Tormead School

THE BATTLE

Two armies opposed,
Each two men deep.
Common men, men on horseback,
Fight alongside churchmen and nobles,
Their castles to defend.
Each side is strong and bold,
Equal in strength and skill.
They plot and plan,
Their moves are well rehearsed,
One step forward,
One step backwards
Two steps sideways.
What fierce fighting!
Bishops sweeping across the battlefield.
A castle is captured,
A queen in danger!
The soldiers huddle round,
Too late, she is gone.
Outwitted and outsmarted.
One .side is sadly depleted,
Their numbers greatly reduced.
The king! The king!
God save the king!
The enemy is advancing,
There is no way out.
Checkmate!

Annabel Dumbreck (12)
Tormead School

MY LITTLE BRO'!

My little bro', he's only three,
He screams and cries,
But he's cute as can be!

The strange thing is
He's really strong,
he'd pick up nearly anyone!

He picks up tanks,
Look, I know,
He can balance a bookcase on one toe.

Last night I saw him in his bed,
With the wardrobe rested on his head!

I don't know why he's really strong,
He beats up me, my dad, my mum!

His knife is now a heavy axe,
He hits his bowl and soon it cracks!

Feeding can be very sore,
And screaming means he wants some more!

He's muscly
I must admit,
He must really be pretty fit!

My little bro',
I love him a lot,
Even though he's been strong,
Ever since he left his cot!

Lucy Milsom (11)
Tormead School

BIRTHDAYS

I always have loved birthdays,
Just like Christmas too,
But there is something about birthdays
That nothing else can do.

Presents are exciting,
I love to see my cake,
My friends are all invited
To come and celebrate.

Sometimes we go swimming
Or picnic in the park,
Once we even had a clown
And fireworks in the dark.

When the day is over
And everyone has gone,
I think about the day I had
And hope the next one won't be long.

Larisa Hammond (12)
Tormead School

WINTER

Cold, frosty air bites my fingers,
Like the hound of winter.
As I step on the frozen puddles,
The icy surface splinters.

Slow are my steps through the deep snow,
And the street lamp lights my way.
The swirling snow burns my eyelids
In the midst of the snowy fray.

As morning comes, Jack Frost has hung
The icicles on the eaves.
Each blade of grass all dressed in white
And the frost encrusts the leaves.

Susie Garrard (12)
Tormead School

THE ENVIRONMENT

Our environment
Was clean and captivating,
Until we humans
Started debating.

The suffering of animals
Has become too grand,
It has become too much
For me to stand.

The pollution has covered
Land, sea and air,
Now there is no room
For people to spare.

The rainforests
Are disappearing,
Then end of nature
Must be nearing.

Some people
Will agree with me.
The world will live happily ever after,
You'll see.

Lara Lemon (11)
Tormead School

BORN FOR FUN

The bundle of fur came running towards me,
It was furry and cute from what I could see,
It had big bright eyes and soft fluffy fur,
Along with a very big engine purr

But surely not this entire kitten was sweet,
After all, the birds it caught did tweet!
Its mother's tail was definitely pulled
And with fake mice the kitten was fooled.

With pouncing and prancing it flew through the air,
But never landed clumsily or without care,
It would be picked up in premonition
For that fear came in a motherly fashion.

Granny's knitting soon to be unfurled,
And her ball of wool would soon be uncurled,
And however cuddly the kittens may be,
I do not think they are the ones for Granny.

Emily Sloper (12)
Tormead School

MINI-ME

Mini-me is only three feet tall,
Even his father thinks he's small.
He walks around in his silver suit
And although he is ugly, he's rather cute.

Mini-me takes his name from his dad,
Who is a bigger version of his lad.
Doctor Evil is the raiser
Of the boy who loves his laser.

Mini-me and his father sing to Scott, the brother,
Their favourite song is like no other,
They do a duet of 'Just the Two of Us',
It makes Scott feel like a wuss.

Mini-me one day will take over
The Evil empire and all its bother.
He's bound to cause a lot of trouble,
His life has been such a muddle.

Isabelle Lomas (11)
Tormead School

THE SEA

It glimmers in the moonlight,
It glistens in the day,
It sways in the afternoon,
It washes your thoughts away.

Time after time it falls over,
Making a calm and gentle sound,
Like the singing of a sparrow on a winter's morn,
In it all kinds of treasures are found.

It is a home to some, but not to others,
To some it is a place of fun and laughter.
Above is a clear, open space,
Allowing winds to blow about the place.

It is a treasure, it is the sea.

Charlotte Boyle (12)
Tormead School

BUTTERFLY

Butterfly,
You fly so high
From the moment that you hatch,
Why are you so hard to catch?
I want to see you up very close,
For it is you that I like most.
I want to study you carefully
And watch your wings flutter merrily.
You amaze me butterfly,
You make me feel high,
With you I could never tell a lie.
One day I *will* catch you butterfly,
When that day should arise,
The air shall be filled with my joyous cries.

Georgina Lunan (11)
Tormead School

WINTER MONTHS

My favourite month is December
As it is so cold and blizzardy.
Making snowmen and snowballs,
Sledging down a hill,
Or sitting by a warm log fire,
Roasting sausages and marshmallows,
And toasting my feet, nice and warm.
I wish it carried on all year.
My favourite day is Christmas Day
As there is fun and games, songs and pressies.

India Sage (11)
Tormead School

AUTUMN

I love the crisp crunch of the new fallen leaves,
As I walk home from school through a path
Of golden seas,
The crowds of children play in the fields,
Having conker wars or battles with leaves,
I can see but a metre in front of my nose,
The chilly autumn breeze eats through my jumper,
But then it starts attacking me,
The smell of bonfires wafts through the air,
As hedgehogs nestle in beds of moss,
While squirrels feast on their abundance of nuts,
But what is this I see? A snowflake,
The snow queen has cast her spell on me.

Alice Guilder (11)
Tormead School

AUTUMN

Ribbons of white braid through the still, blue sky.
The majestic beech tree is crowned with golden leaves.
Whilst the sun shimmers through its gilded canopy,
Gently, slow, the dry rusty leaves glide to the ground through
the smoky mist.
Amber leaves lounging, layer upon layer, around the tree.
The crisp frost coats the leaves in a shawl of silver.
Sprightly, sharply, the squirrel scrambles up the tree rustling
the dry leaves.
The leaves fall, swooping and swaying to settle on the frosty layer.
Golden stars on a silver shroud.

Kate Eglinton (11)
Tormead School

WHAT IS IT?

She is black and white
She never bites,
Her bright green eyes at night
Give me a fright.

She plays ping-pong
All day long,
Or she catches a mouse
And brings it to the house.

Her large paws
And sharp claws,
Help her to get stuck in a tree
Or caught in trouble with a bumblebee.

Have you guessed?
Because you'll get in a mess,
But she's my cat
Who never wants a chat!

Sarah Flaxman (11)
Tormead School

AUTUMN

Crispy, golden leaves crunch under my feet,
Gold, bronze, red and pink,
Some still green from the spring,
Trees around me losing their leaves.

Birds singing their mystical autumn songs,
Swifts preparing to fly south for warmth,
Blackbirds eating red and golden berries,
Squirrels snuggling down to hibernate.

In the misty coldness of autumn,
My breath is tiny puffs in the cold, fresh air.
The ground still wet from the dew,
Jack Frost whitening the green grass.

Clare Coley (11)
Tormead School

A PERFECT DAY

Golden sand
Glistening in the sun,
Only me there,
First footprints of the day,
Soft sand between my toes.

The sea is calm,
Like a lake on a quiet day,
Waves ripple gently on the shore,
A fishing boat bobbing on the horizon.

Beautiful rock pools,
The water glittering in the sun,
Tiny shells shine like jewels,
Buried treasure lies beneath.

Sea anemones, star fish,
Baby crabs, tiny prawns,
Seaweed floating,
Hiding the secrets below.

As I dip my toes in
The fish dart from pool to pool,
Weaving in and out of the seaweed.
Crabs scurry under stones.

Sophie Jebb (11)
Tormead School

THE AUTUMN BREEZE

You can hear it in the rustling trees,
It's cold and fierce, the autumn breeze.
It catches you with a shiver,
It makes you shake and quiver.

It's never seen,
It's only heard,
It is like a large, gliding bird.

The minute you can hear it pass,
The autumn comes so very fast.
The leaves turn a golden brown,
And then they start to tumble down

And with one almighty blow,
The breeze turns into winter snow.

Saskia Frost (11)
Tormead School

COLOURS

Black is a grumpy grown-up,
Grey is a wet, windy day,
Red is a fiery five-year old who wants to have his own way.

Green is the growing grass of the countryside,
Brown is the contented purr of the cat,
Blue is the slippy slide of a bubbling stream,
Wearing the river bed flat.

Orange is the copper colour of autumn,
Yellow, a sunny summer's day,
Gold is the colour of sunrise at dawn on a morning in May.

Silver is the gleaming glow of the moon when the clouds
Get in the way,
Black, as night, returns again at the end of the day.

Sophie Garrett (11)
Tormead School

RABBITS

I love rabbits,
I have two at home,
With their noses they absorb every smell,
And their sharp ears that catch every sound,
And their white tails that flick if there's danger.

I love rabbits,
I have two at home,
They play all day,
They hop up and down,
That's all they do.

I love rabbits,
I have two at home,
One sleeps all day,
One *bites!*
But they are really cuddly.

I love rabbits, I have two at home.

Laura Cowper (11)
Tormead School

GHOST TEACHER

The moon is high,
The night is black,
The school is deserted,
And full of bats.
The staff have fled,
All the children are gone,
But the ghost of a teacher lingers on.

She enters the school
Which is empty and unstaffed,
And opens her classroom
To an absent class.
She opens her briefcase,
Cobwebbed and dusty,
And calls the register
To her vacant class.

She then packs her briefcase
And waves 'goodbye',
And puts on her coat,
Worn, but dry.
Closing the door
She exits the classroom,
Walks along the corridor
To sit in the staffroom.

The moon is high,
The night it black,
The school is deserted
And full of rats.
The staff have fled,
All the children are gone,
But the ghost of a teacher lingers on.

Lizzy Von Schweinitz (11)
Tormead School

A Winter's Night

The sun sets, it is night,
The stars start to twinkle,
The snowflakes start falling like dancing ballerinas,
Then the snow starts to fall, soon,
Everything is covered in snow, everything is white.
The animals are asleep, the humans are asleep.
It is silent, beautifully silent.
Then in the distance, there is a burst of light,
The sun rises,
The glistening stars fade away, the animals awaken.
The sun gleams on the snow,
It is now a winter's morning, just a winter's morning.

Helen Rance (12)
Tormead School

Autumn

Autumn marks the season of chaos!
Reds, orange, bronze and browns are the colours of death.
Autumn is the messenger of winter.
He erupts the plants circle of life and the winds thrust out
their lungs to damage the world.
Autumn whips the life out of you and me with its sharp, cold claws!
Featherlike dandelions tell the fortune of the year 2000!
Autumn assassinates summer as autumn is the god of murder and
summer is the goddess of the new.
Majorcan Jazmine is cut and slaughtered in the heavy hands of autumn.
Silently only the roses can be left standing in the *world!*

Martine Wilson (11)
Tormead School

CHRISTMAS ICING

The waterfall of the crisp white snow,
The crunching under the boots,
The prickly Christmas holly,
The coldness of the winter's air.

The crackling of the burning log fire,
The laughs of children playing,
The drifting scent of pine needles,
The stomping of feet upstairs.

The scrunching and crunching of Christmas paper,
The pops and bangs of crackers,
The beaming light of the moon shining down,
Now everything's quiet . . . except one,

The clock,
Tick-tock, tick-tock, tick-tock.

Harriet Kopij (11)
Tormead School

DREAMS AND NIGHTMARES

Dreams are very strange,
They can be happy,
They can be sad,
But they can turn people fairly mad.

Nightmares are these horrible dreams
That wake you in the middle of the night
With a cold sweat and a terrible fright.

But we should forget about these scary dreams
And think about more pleasantries.
For example an ideal dream would be . . .
Living the life of luxury.

Matilda Baker (11)
Tormead School

SEAGULL

Soaring, soaring,
Higher and higher,
Above the sea,
Below the sky.

As I wonder,
Every day,
Is there any
Food to spare.

I look to the shore,
There's no one there.
I look to the sea,
It's empty too.

The wind's picked up,
I'm getting cold,
I'm all alone,
But I'm still . . .

Soaring, soaring,
Higher and higher,
Above the sea,
Below the sky.

Alana Johnson (11)
Tormead School

The Year - Seasons

White is the colour of winter,
Fresh is the smell of a cold winter's morn,
The snow everywhere is what you can see,
The squawk of the robin is what you can hear,
On a cold winter's day.

Green is the colour of spring,
The bulbs sprouting up everywhere,
New baby animals everywhere,
You can feel the soft fur
Of their mums.

Yellow is the colour of summer,
The bright summer sun shining down,
You can taste the fresh air
And the fruit from the orchard trees
Which once lay bare.

Orange is the colour of autumn,
The leaves turn brown, crimson and gold.
The leaves in the orchard start to fall
And at the end of the season are bare once again.

You can smell winter coming
And we start once again,
Through winter, spring, summer and autumn.
The bulbs pop through,
The trees start to grow their food once again
To feed us for another year.

Alice Hewitt (11)
Tormead School

THE SEA

My journey never began,
And it shall never end,
For my soul is immortal,
And my spirit free.

In the morning
The glorious sun rises over me,
The white horses gallop to their destiny,
And I am free.

And even when the moon's radiant face
Dances across mine,
And the stars shine so brightly,
And you shall be sleeping,
And I am still free

The eerie silence
And the creeping mist surround me,
The waves leap in silvery ribbons from their sleep,
And I am still free.

And only when you can paint
With all the colours of the wind,
You can be as free as me,
Wild at heart.

For my soul is immortal
And my spirit free.

Eleanor Purkhardt (11)
Tormead School

THE STARING DRAGON

The dragon awoke
After 100 years,
The dragon awoke,
He had no fears.

He sniffed and
Wrinkled his nose
And spiders had nested
Between his toes.

Had anyone been there?
Had any one dared?
When last time they looked,
A dragon had glared?

Bump, clump,
Bump, clump.

He stiffened
And stared
And if you looked,
His teeth were bared.

He stared but
Saw nothing,
He sniffed but
Smelt nothing.

Bump, clump.
Bump, clump.

The footsteps got nearer,
Bump, clump,
Who'd want to walk here
In this type of dump?

Bump, clang, thump,
The Dragon looked,
Bump, clang, thump,
A man looked.

The dragon stood
Not moving a muscle,
He didn't attack,
No hustle and bustle.

The dragon was a statue,
Not moving, not breathing.
Bump, clump, bump,
Away from the dump.

Verena Partridge (12)
Tormead School

HONEYBEE

Little, furry, black and yellow,
Bumbling, flying cosy jackets,
Bombing, diving into flowers,
Gathering nectar, zooming hivewards,
Feelers twitching, waving, swaying,
Alert for dangers stirring, moving,
Wings vibrating, buzzing, humming,
Urging other bees to follow.

Eleanor Grieveson (11)
Tormead School

POSTCARDS FROM HEAVEN

Send me a postcard from heaven,
From way up there in the sky.
Send me a postcard from heaven,
From where the rain falls on high.
Send me a postcard from heaven
From where the sun shimmers so bright,
Send me a postcard from heaven,
From where the moon glistens at night.

Send me a postcard from heaven,
from way up there in the sky,
Send me a postcard from heaven,
From where the stars and planets lie.
Send me a postcard from heaven,
From up there with the clouds and blue,
Send me a postcard from heaven,
From where you have the best views.

Send me a postcard from heaven,
From way up there in the sky,
Send me a postcard from heaven,
From where you have gone to lie,
Send me a postcard from heaven,
If only you could see me now,
Send me a postcard from heaven,
I know that you would be proud.

Send me a postcard from heaven,
From way up there in the sky,
Send me a postcard from heaven,
From where the rain falls on high,
Send me a postcard from heaven,
I have sat alone and wondered why,
Why I never got to say 'goodbye'.

Laura Young (12)
Tormead School

THE CHRISTMAS CASTLE

It stands up tall,
a brilliant green,
laid upon a winter scene.
The staircase twists and doesn't stop,
It's hours before you reach the top.
There's doors galore and so much more,
There's lots to see I'm very sure.
The soldiers guard both day and night,
Dressed in cherry-red velvet and fluffy crisp white.
A thousand princesses float down from their strings,
In long, golden dresses and elegant wings.
Coloured lights illuminate the glowing corridors
And reach into every single place on a million floors.
Instead of a painting there is a glittering jewel
At every single place,
To give the walls some colour
Which reflects upon your face.
Fireworks of colour spring into the sky,
Catching all attention
As past you they fly by.
And finally the queen who sits upon her throne
At the very top,
Is dressed in gold and silver and sits there all alone.
But the people of her castle sing and sing and sing,
She listens to them all
And the happiness they bring.

Tara Davies (11)
Tormead School

THE FOOT OF THE MOUNTAIN GOAT

The wind is alive with the bite of the frost,
The ground is afresh with the powdery snow,
The trees droop down with the weight of the ice,
This world is quieter than the quietest night,
For no creature dare, with its furry coat,
Wander these lands, but the foot of the mountain goat.

The whistle and wail of the wind through the trees,
The pitter-patter of the snowflakes coming to rest,
The trickle of the tiny stream as it weaves its way down
the mountainside,
No human will ever experience these sounds,
For no creature dare, with its furry coat,
Wander these lands, but the foot of the mountain goat.

The glowing warmth that comes from within,
When the noise dies down, and the peace fills in,
Every smell, every sound, every sight you might see,
To the door of these feelings, you won't find a key,
For no creature dare, with its furry coat,
Wander these lands, but the foot of the mountain goat.

Nicola Pocock (12)
Tormead School

CHERRY

Her chestnut coat gleaming,
Her bright eyes glint in the sun,
Her mane flowing freely
As she gallops up the run.

Her gallop is like a drum beat,
As fast as the wind,
The three socks on her feet
As white as snow had been.

Her movement is very steady,
Just like a rocking horse,
She is always ready
To gallop with full force.

Sophie Callender (13)
Tormead School

WAITING FOR WINTER

I can't wait till winter comes,
The long winter walks,
I wrap up warm and with my family we venture into
the frosty afternoon.
The trees are bare, dancing in the chilly wind.
The wind slashes against my face,
It makes my soft cheeks red, as red as a garden apple
That glows in the autumn sun.
Waiting for winter.

Sitting in the small, cosy lounge, drinking hot tea
And eating toasted teacakes.
We warm frozen toes by the fire.
Wrapping the presents in bright paper, putting them under the tree,
Counting how many are sitting there ready for me.
Making Christmas puddings, stirring and making a wish.
Collecting holly and ivy,
Buying the Christmas tree.
Putting up the mistletoe in the sheltered lamp-lit porch,
Longing for winter.

The thick, white duvet covers all.
Bulbs and seeds tucked safely in the bed beneath.
Waiting for spring.

Grace Williams (11)
Tormead School

HODGEHEG!

Hodgeheg the hedgehog
Is very long-snouted and
Loves worms, slugs and snails.

Poor Mister Hodgeheg's
Hearing and eyesight is poor,
But he has keen smell.

Hodgeheg has short ears
And a brown, spiny body
Which is quite prickly.

Hodge sleeps all day
In a burrow until night,
When he is most active.

To protect himself,
He scrunches into a ball
And sticks his spines out.

In autumn, Hodgeheg
Collects lots of leaves and food
For hibernation.

Hodge sleeps in a ball,
Through winter till spring,
When the sun warms him.

Gemma Blake (11)
Tormead School

SEASONS

The seasons go fluttering by,
Without a sound, without a care.

Spring is lively, colourful and bright,
And quite warm compared to cold winter nights.
But be warned, it can be wet too,
So make sure that you take a raincoat with you!
Spring smells like honey, sweet in the air,
I think it is lovely, and I'm glad that it's there!

Summer is warm, pretty and fun,
With lots of games to play in the summer sun.
There's sprinklers and hoses and holidays too,
Plus much, much more for everybody to do.
Summer has an aroma of flowers and perfume,
It really is a lovely season, don't you think so too?

Autumn is cold, with leaves fluttering down,
And all different colours, like red, gold and brown.
You can build a huge leaf pile then scatter it around,
Or count all the leaves that are lying on the ground,
Autumn has a smell of wet leaves and grass,
And if it took an exam I'd give it a pass.

Winter is freezing, with ice everywhere,
And maybe even snowflakes that fall on your hair.
You could, though, build snowmen, if there was enough snow,
But you'd have to wear gloves and a scarf for that you know.
Winter smells like water, ice and wet wood,
But I can see that it is nice, and I think that you should.

The seasons go fluttering by,
Without a sound, without a care.

Philippa Goldenberg (11)
Tormead School

TIME

Through the swirling mists of time,
I look and wonder,
What does the future hold for me?
Where shall I go?
What will I be?

I think of the past,
And I feel so lucky,
That I should be happy,
That I should be free.

I feel the present,
My friends all around,
All that I like,
Somewhere near can be found.

The long lanes of the past
Are left far behind.

The present to work.

And the future
To find.

Charlie Heslop (11)
Tormead School

MAY

In May I go walking,
Listening to the wonderful sounds of May.
The slight sound of the blowing trees,
The birds in the morning chirping so happily
In their favourite time of the year.
There is laughter, happiness and joy everywhere.

In May I go walking, smelling
The beautiful smells of May.
The flowers coming out have tremendous smells.
I smell that freshness in the air.
There is laughter, happiness and joy everywhere.

Natasha Hoban (11)
Tormead School

MR CHOCOLATE

At eight o'clock on Friday morning
The chocolate monster wakes up yawning,
He goes around Chocolate Town
In his mud brown chocolate gown,
Spreading chocolate, toffee and sweets
To all the people that he meets,
Then he goes to Wonka's factory
And gets his wages (which are satisfactory!),
That are mainly confectionery
And that makes him very, very merry,
All his friends are very happy
And towards him they are never snappy.

Choc chip,
Apple pip,
Milky bears,
Chocolate pears,
He gives out
To every pout,
Until one day
He got tooth decay!

Vanessa Fowler Kendall (11)
Tormead School

ORANGE

Orange is summer,
The bright burning sun.
People are swimming
While having great fun.

Orange is autumn,
Leaves floating down,
Like bright little angels,
In orange are crowned.

Orange is winter,
The fires are warm.
They burn all the night,
Right through to dawn.

Orange is spring,
The new sweet, fresh flowers.
The small sleepy hedgehog
Awakens and cowers.

Katherine Fowler (11)
Tormead School

WINTER

W   hen it is winter it is dull and the trees are bare,
I   t is frosty everywhere, the street is like a white cloud,
N   o one is ever playing down the street because it is cold,
T   rees are being shook by the fierce wind,
E   ngines of cars won't start because of the icy snow,
R   amblers are walking on muddy hills in one row.

Sarah Calvard (11)
Tormead School

TRICK OR TREAT MORTISHA

It started months and months ago,
When amid the summer sun,
I did something I do every year,
When the time is getting near,
I start to plan my Hallowe'en costume.

This year I planned to be Mortisha,
With a long black dress and long black hair,
I was going 'trick or treating',
I was going with Jamie and Louise,
I began to draw my Hallowe'en costume.

I made up the face, a face as white as a sheet,
I made the dress, a dress as black as ebony,
I made the hair, the hair as black as night,
I made the hand, the thing I'd had to make,
With all that done I donned by Hallowe'en costume.

We drove through blackness,
The darkness, the gloom,
The place where Macbeth's witches would loom,
We drove through the night with cats' eyes on the road,
And at last we arrived at Gosterwood Manor.

We drove down the path to whining and wailing,
We arrived at the house that was towering above us,
That slightly resembled the Adams' family house,
I was greeted at the door by Wednesday and Gomez,
What happened next? You'll never know!

Frederica Byron (11)
Tormead School

It's Winter

When the snowflakes skim across the thick grey sky,
And the cold, sharp wind bites at people's faces and fingers,
And icicles drip from the window sill,
It's winter.

When a thin, white blanket covers the world,
And no flowers grow in the garden.
When people wear warm and woolly wraps,
It's winter.

When Jack Frost dances on the windowpane,
And the glass shatters like ice beneath your feet,
And fires roar to keep us warm,
It's winter.

When the animals sleep in a leafy bed,
And the birds fly away for the winter.
When a nasty cold keeps you indoors,
It's winter.

When carol singers knock at your door,
And we eat roasted chestnuts and mince pies.
When Christmas pantomimes are performed,
It's winter.

When happy children run out to make snowmen,
And have snowball fights and races,
And the whistling wind accompanies them in their cry,
It's winter.

Rosamund Hatfield (11)
Tormead School

FIREWORK NIGHT

Crackle, sizzle and spit
Red, orange flames
Hot, bright exploding fire
Thick smoke flowing up
Bright, shooting, exploding
Fireworks blasting in the darkness
Banging, darting out
Pink, orange, green
Sparkling in the midnight sky
Reaching up
Shattering into pieces
Flying into unknown sky
Glittering with colour
Red, purple, blue
Amazement spreads
Children gasping at
The magnificent sight
Afraid of the sparks of light
Dying down
Ashes spread
Flames gasp for breath
Their life is coming to an end
Stillness has arrived
No noise to be heard
Firework night has ended.

Kate St Hill (12)
Tormead School

SNOWFLAKES

As they gently fall through the air,
They glide swiftly, without a care,
Their delicate details shine in the light,
You watch them as they start their flight.

They tumble and soar and flutter through the sky,
They are just as beautiful as a golden butterfly,
Their craftsmanship, like a spider's web so fine,
Oh how I wish, they were all mine.

They are a silvery white like a frozen lake,
They are so perfect, no mistakes,
You wish that you could join them in the sky,
And dance and dance till morning is nigh.

But why when you hold out your hand,
They mystically disappear
And end their wonderful journey?

Francesca Rozwadowska (13)
Tormead School

WINTER

Winter is when I watch snow falling
from my bedroom window,
I can see it gently floating to the ground
making a beautiful bright white carpet.

Winter is when I feel cold air
all over me,
It seems to make my fingers shrink
and my feet go numb.

Winter is when I throw snowballs
at my friends,
at my mum,
at my dog,
at everyone.

Winter is when I enjoy nice hot roasts
which make my body feel warm,
I eat them up in no time at all,
and then I want some more.

Jenny Barker (11)
Tormead School

MY DREAM FOR THE MILLENNIUM - MUSIC FROM THE STARS

In the silence of the night
Gentle music is heard,
Is there something up there, is it a bird?
It flaps its giant wings,
It hums a quiet song,
The world is peaceful, there is no wrong.
It changed our way of thinking,
It changed the unhappy war,
It changed us completely, it opened a new door.
Now our world is peaceful,
The dazzling dragon flies above,
Hidden in the dark of night,
Like a gentle dove.

Katrina Scott (11)
Tormead School

DEATH

We had dinner with them last night,
Her Swiss smile looked a bit shy,
As she gazed out of her young crinkly eyes.
Today, she's warm, bubbly, full of love and life,
Her shyness overcome by all that.

We had visited Longwood Gardens,
Physically unable to absorb the thousands of orchids, cacti and palms,
We had laughed and told stories, she told us of hibiscus at her home,
And she told us of her home in Nigeria
Where she worked as a nurse 'in the bush'.

Jenni is full of humour, she looks, laughs, tells stories,
How can she have acute leukaemia - right now as we talk together?
Today she's fine, she is in remission,
But she will be fortunate to live a month or two.
She will leave behind her dreams, achievements and family.

I remember Jenni long before the diagnosis,
The unique magic displayed in her eyes, especially after meeting Alex.
At school she was the envy of us all – she had it all, money, looks,
                                                      boys and fame.
She never felt she'd really die. The pain almost crushes her,
But she stands bravely against the expected,
Putting the needs of others before hers as she stares death in the eyes.

Today, I'm grateful for a friend like Jenni,
She made my life bearable and brighter
Even when death's spear impaled.
Even when walking towards death and leaving everything she loved,
She was still Jenni, strong, courageous and above all, caring.

So please don't feel alienated from death.
When it happens you take no chances thinking 'Could have been me!'
But later you forget, 'cause it never is – it's always someone else.
You always escape, till you don't!
And the world just keeps moving on and on –
Not even death can change that.

Moni Oladapo (13)
Tormead School

FIREWORKS AND BONFIRES

Autumn is a colourful time of year,
All reds, yellows, browns and golds,
I often hear the crunch of leaves and
Sometimes the bangs of fireworks.
I often see in the distance
Lots of fireworks in the sky,
And sometimes I see
The smoke from an odd bonfire.
We have a bonfire every year,
It crackles and spits galore,
But if I get too near
I become burnt on the spot.
I love to step on the leaves
And hear the crunch it makes,
I like collecting all kinds of leaves,
And pressing them so they keep
But although I like all that,
I think I prefer summer,
I can go out and play
In the rays of the sun!

Rebecca Moore (11)
Tormead School

LEAVES

Swirling, twisting, turning,
Floating down below.
Whirling, twirling, circling
Where do they all go?
Flittering, turning
Across the land.
Wittering, circling
Over the sand.

Red and gold and yellow
All the colours that I see.
Auburn and green and mellow
They are as beautiful as can be.
Brown and yellow
Gently swaying in the wind.
Lime and mellow
Just before the ground will freeze.

The leaves that fall in autumn.

Rebecca Atkinson (11)
Tormead School

A WINTER'S DAY

Warm fire burning,
Outside bright white,
The Christmas tree's decorations shine,
The dog barking outside.

Roast turkey cooking,
Smoky chimneys outside,
Mince pie on the table,
The train whizzing by.

Screaming of children,
Snowballs in the air,
My cosy warm bed,
The smell of Christmas pudding.

Christmas presents around the tree,
I hope they're all for me,
Outside the sledge is parked,
Waiting for us to tumble down the hill.

Eleanor Horton (12)
Tormead School

AUTUMN

Brown, yellow, red and gold,
falling slowly in the cold.
Flittering here and fluttering there,
never stopping in the air.
Pumpkins with that orangey glow,
air so cold it sends shivers down your toe.
Looking over there on the hills far away,
I see the multicoloured carpet winding east,
                    then north far into the horizon.
Fireworks light up the evening sky,
glittering purple, then blue up there so high.
Here in the woods the trees grow bare,
and the hare is caught fast in the snare.
When the sun sinks down on this lonely place
with a gleaming glow on that golden face.
Going down, down, sinking onto the horizon until . . .
                    it . . .
                        disappears!

Francesca Thompson (11)
Tormead School

THE STEAM TRAIN TO MALLAIG

Here we are awaiting
the arrival of the train
as the rattle of the engines
gets louder and nearer and clearer.

We step inside
the quaking carriages
ready to begin.
The tiring ride to Mallaig
has only just begun.

The piercing scream of the whistle
says we're all set to go.
As we wave goodbye to the station
the journey is underway.

I can hear the wind rushing past
as we zoom along the tracks.
The roaring of the engine
sounds like a fierce, hungry lion
chasing after his terrified prey.

The train is slowing down now
and it pulls up to the station.
All the passengers rushing past me
searching for a door.

As I glance around behind me
expecting to see the train
I see nothing but a puff of smoke.
But then I hear the whistle
calling a final goodbye.

Philippa Rush (11)
Tormead School

GHOSTS

Drifting through the darkness:
A misty white they glow,
But where they've been
And what they've seen
No one will ever know.

Their shrill scream will torment you
Through the blackness of the night,
But don't dare move
Or you may prove
The undead live tonight.

Their chill will move all through you,
Send shivers through your heart.
You'll never heal,
They'll make you feel
Your fear, tear you apart.

Is your imagination
Telling you lies tonight?
Or is it true
That they kill you
By shock at their mere sight?

The cold breeze on your collar
Which scares us all the most;
Unfinished deeds,
And ghastly needs -
Are you afraid of ghosts?

Jackie Walbank (13)
Tormead School

SHADES OF NIGHT

Grey clouds slide in from the west,
The once blue sky is getting dressed.
The sun disappears, too shy to come out,
Nocturnal animals are now about;
The barn owl hoots and toots with might,
Little mice scurry back out for the night.
The moon appears and shows her face,
Installing herself in the sun's warm place.
Nestled in the sky she whiles the night away,
Till grey clouds return to hide her from the day.

Holly Winton (13)
Tormead School

CHOCOLATE!

As brown as mud, as sticky as toffee,
As sweet as sugar, and very yummy.
The irresistible taste makes my mouth mumble,
And makes my tummy rumble, for more and more.
The heavenly smell, makes me feel dreamy,
The luxurious feel inside, makes me feel sleepy.
So eat this treat, and break off a block,
Of heavenly smelling . . . chocolate!

Cassie Hall (11)
Tormead School

THE LONER

I am always alone - no one likes me,
I hide in the corner - no one wants me,
It is like I am invisible - no one sees me,
I have always been a loner and always will be.

It's four-thirty and I'm alone,
My classmates are playing rounders and they
                              are picking the teams,
I sneak into the line not hoping to be seen,
By the end of the match my frown will be a beam.

Joan and Mike are popular it seems,
'I'll take Jack,' 'I'll take Sarah,' they shout and scream,
Then I'm alone - the last in line,
They are not letting me in, I knew they would not be kind.

I turn away trying to fight back tears,
Then I feel one on my cheek, I can hear cheering near,
If only those cheers were for me, just once,
Then I wouldn't be a loner, well at least not much.

I open the great black door of my house,
My mum's on the phone, she is never anywhere else,
'Mum,' I ask, 'can I talk to you for a minute?'
'Later dear, later dear, I'm on the phone to your Aunt Nibit.'

I trail upstairs with tears spilling down my face,
They feel like fire in a cold, cold place,
Oh, why can't anyone like me, why can't I have a friend?
Will I be a loner forever?
Will I be a loner until the end?

Laura Cheetham (11)
Tormead School

STOLEN

Remembering old times,
With an aching pain in my heart,
I never imagined it could be over,
I never wanted to be apart.

His pale, red lips,
His tanned complexion,
I can't stop loving him,
It's out of the question.

His mousy brown hair,
His warm and relaxed smile,
His gentle and innocent eyes,
Can no longer stare at me from across the isle.

Minutes to hours,
Hours to days,
Time passes so slowly,
I can't carry on this way.

Looking down at your grave, trying to be strong,
The wind blows my hair as I turn to walk away,
Always remaining in my heart,
I swear you will stay.

Khatidja Janmohamed (14)
Tormead School

FIREWORK NIGHT

The sky ablaze with colour,
The flashes of bright light,
The Catherine wheels spinning,
Leaving patterns in the night.

The rockets soaring upwards,
Bangers whizzing on the ground,
The sizzle of the fire,
The air is filled with sound.

People stamping on the ground,
Trying to keep warm,
While brightly coloured rockets
Go flying across the lawn.

Children stuff Guy Fawkes with hay,
And throw him on the flames,
The ooos and ahhs come from the crowd
As out flows golden rain.

We write our names with sparklers,
The fun will never end.
But the last firework lights the sky,
Then darkness falls again.

Gabriella Jarvis (14)
Tormead School

THE DOG

His ears twitched as I called his name,
His tail wagged as he turned to look at me,
He started to run,
He had to get that ball.

His ears flapped as he ran,
His tail wagged furiously,
He ran like the wind,
He had to get that ball.

His ears were out of control,
His tail no longer mattered,
His eyes had a look of desperation in them,
He had to get that ball.

His ears twitched again,
His tail slowed down,
He stopped running,
He did not care about the ball any longer.

He turned slowly,
His tail no longer wagging,
His eyes looked troubled,
What had he heard?

There was a deadly silence,
Everyone in the park turned to look,
People screamed, running madly,
But the dog did not understand.

He aimed and fired,
A smile appeared faintly on his lips,
It hit the dog above his eyes; he hit the ground,
The dog was dead.

Laura Nash (13)
Tormead School

A STALLION ON THE AMERICAN PLAINS

Standing there, head to the wind,
Mane swept back in the chilly breeze.
With good strong hocks and a kindly eye,
With ears which almost touch the sky.
Bold and wise he stands on a rock,
Jutting out from the steep hill's top
Seeing all, hearing all.

Yells of distant riders,
Distant thundering hooves,
Getting closer, ever closer.
He takes it in, not stirring an inch -
Who are they to invade his territory,
Invading his land, his plains?
Disturbing his privacy.

In his eye a flame flickers,
And from his herd a mare whickers
Yet he does not move.
He knows the riders' sole intention,
Knows the danger with which he is threatened
Whirling ropes and glinting spurs –
Coming upon him,
Yet still he stays.

Then, with a flick of his tail
And a kick of his heels,
And a signal to his mares to run -
He is gone, shimmering gold,
back down to where he belongs.

Georgina Coleby (13)
Tormead School

MY BEST FRIEND

He's barking mad! they say
Ha ha, get it - barking!
But I don't care what they think.

Ooh! He smells, they'll screech.
That musty towel smell, mouldy, dog stench.
But I don't care what they think.

He's only an ignorant mongrel
What would he know?
But I don't care what they think.

He is so much smarter than they'll ever be
And more sensitive that they'll ever know.
But I don't care what they think.

He doesn't have feelings
Or a brain, they say.
But I don't care what they think.

They can keep all their toy dogs
I'd rather have a friend than a prize-winner.
So I don't care what they think.

He's my best friend
They can't change that, no matter what they say.
So I don't care what they think.

Stephanie Dean (13)
Tormead School

THROUGH THE SHADOWS

Through the shadows of the midnight sky
I felt it coming as I passed by
Weary and alone, I glimpsed to the right
And like a flash it was out of sight.

On the terrace where it first begun
I dined where the mistletoe hung
A swift breeze like no other before
Swept right past me and slammed the door.

Cold and afraid, I sat in silence
But fear and dread is no alliance
I picked up the chair and flung it in the black
But only to see it flying right back.

This was no joke, my house was haunted
Goodness me, I felt quite daunted
Bearing it no longer, I locked it away
Only to find it back the next day.

Evacuating my house achieved nothing
Until I found out about something
A priest could send this spirit away
In less than a week or even a day.

A year later, I had settled down
In a nice old flat on the outskirts of town
Falling asleep, my stomach churned
I knew it, yes, I knew it, the spirit had returned!

Betty Gasson (13)
Tormead School

DREAMLAND

Dreamland is a place where everyone goes,
When they're warm and snug and wriggling their toes,
Dreamland is a place not hard to find,
Drift off, relax, images in mind.

Colours flashing, bright and bold,
Circling my mind like a story untold,
A circus I see with tigers and bears,
Crashing oceans and winding stairs.

Some water I came to, with a rainbow so bright,
Open my eyes and it was still night,
Closed again, drifting away -
Far away - to yet another day.

Where hippos dance around wheels,
Jokers on top clicking their heels,
Lying there on a bed of roses,
A maiden sleeps surrounded by posies.

A startling blue sky, unicorns in flight,
Fairies flee from a dashing white knight,
Little frogs hop while giants awake,
There are rocks to shift and stones to rake.

Rain pours down, thunder crashes,
Dark clouds gather, lightning flashes,
The world is set and shining bright,
The sun appears as golden light.

You're there now, deep in dreams,
Striking visions and crazy scenes,
It was quite simple, not as I planned,
Now start your adventure in Dreamland.

Louise Godding (14)
Tormead School

MIRROR MIRROR

As I look into the mirror, blue, I see my reflection,
My ashen complexion, red glossy lips and dark eyes, like bored holes
in the expanse of my face - framed by a mass of dull hair.
This is all that the people see - this is my outside, my shell
But as the mirror reflects my face, my face does not reflect my
personality.
For I am not just a face as some may find me,
I am not my face.
So many different things to so many different people,
And another different person to myself and to myself alone.
For I am the only one who knows all of the people that I am,
I may not like all of them, but that, I cannot help.
I am a happy, jovial clown, overtaken by crazy joy, conveying joy
to others,
I am a lustful rose happy to be plucked and used as a decoration,
I am a lost ghost of a soul wandering through the dusty, unused
corridors of my life,
I am a slave of others, willing to do anything to be popular
and to be recognised,
I am a still and silent pool, depthless and reflecting,
I am a moody, forbidding mountainside, rainswept and uninhabitable,
I am a lonely, lost, meandering river, aimlessly winding its way
through barren lands,
I am all and none of these things,
I am everything and nothing.
Who am I?

Mirror, mirror on the wall,
Who is the simplest soul of all?

Katy Gregory-Smith (13)
Tormead School

A TYPICAL DAY AT THE SEASIDE

The sun is seeping through the morning clouds
The waves are lapping against the shore
And as time comes, so come the busy crowds
The people babble, the seagulls caw

The sky turns blue as the clouds clear away
Among the crowds, seagulls search for scraps
The parents try to relax, the youngsters play
The old folk take well-needed naps

Toddlers and babies play in the sand
Parasols are spread across the beach
Couples of all ages walk hand in hand
Waves seem to chase children just out of their reach

Lifeguards on the lookout, watching from their tower
Looking casual, with binoculars in hand
A new one, on the hour, every hour
With a glance, they scour across the golden sand

As the glowing sun sinks into the ocean
And all the people pack up and go
Once again, on the beach, there is no motion
The sea is calm, the sun is low

No longer the sun burns, nor do the waves crash
A certain grey colour falls across the sky
Warm reds and oranges, then suddenly a flash
The seagulls give out their last piercing cry.

Virginia Hobson (13)
Tormead School

RED

Red is the colour of warmth:
Fire burning in the winter,
Cheeks red from frostbite,
Sleepless nights lead to red eyes.

Red was the colour of England:
Traditional red phone boxes,
The stripes in the Union Jack.

Red is the colour of Christmas:
Red berries on the holly bush,
Santa's bright red suit.

Red is the colour of wheat fields:
Red poppies swaying in the breeze,
The stripe of red sky-high above.

Red is the colour of St Valentine's Day:
Red foil-wrapped chocolates,
Red hearts as the symbol of love.

Little red brick houses,
All lined up in rows,
With red roses in the garden.

Red is the colour of the devil,
With his red pointed tail.
Red is the colour of blood,
Flowing through our veins.

Red, a primary colour,
A simple colour.

Natasha Shoult (12)
Tormead School

The Difference Between My Kittens

I love the way,
They're so different.
They look exactly the same.
One patiently waits,
To be fed.
The other screams.
One walks so elegantly,
The other unbalanced and clumsy.
One is lazy,
The other playful.
One waits to be stroked,
The other does everything for your attention.
One sleeps in the sun,
And shows her chocolate-brown hairs.
The other stays cosy inside.
One quietly, politely,
Sleeps on my bed.
The other jumps around and wakes me up.
One hunts everything she sees,
The other minds her business.
One always comes up to me,
The other always runs away.
One purrs when I hold her,
The other keeps a frown.
It's strange the way,
They're so different.
Though they look exactly the same.

Jessica Eilts (12)
Tormead School

SNOW

When in my bedroom,
on the second floor,
I stare outside.
The refreshing snow is slowly drifting,
from a threatening, grey sky,
then slowly settling,
on the thin, hard ground.

Children build snowmen,
with black buttons, scarves and hats,
with carrot noses.
Pawprints in freshly fallen snow,
along hills, paths and streets
while animals shiver.

I see many mothers,
who wrap children up so warmly:
with woolly mittens and bulky coats.
Children love
snow more than sun:
they toboggan down steep hills
and ski on slopes.

I find it sad
when the snow melts,
it seems to disappear,
so no more snowball fights!
I must dream until
another year.

Semini Sumanasuriya (12)
Tormead School

CROCODILE

Crocodile, in your beautiful lake,
As green-robed as a thick, prickly gorse bush,
You are, reptile,
Devil-hued, flat footed.
God has granted you for life,
Lordship of the swamp.

Two skills keep you from drowning:
Splendid gifts granted to you.
You are a master killer!
Look at your skill on the lake;
You are able to plunge,
Deep down to the bottom of the river,
Glancing up, ugly green reptile,
To survey the earth's surface,
Scanning the lake floor below,
Collecting food like a hunter.
You ride the waves superbly,
To waylay creatures.
Your weapons, ugly creature,
are your sharp and vicious teeth.
Keeper of the oval swamp,
breast the colour of sand,
You look ugly in the colourful jungle,
In a green shirt,
A doublet, a thousand leaves,
A jacket of bushes,
You are the bad one among reptiles,
Green-cloaked, a reptile of hell.

Alice Aram (12)
Tormead School

THE SNAKE

Who's that, slithering, sliding along
his tail rattling in the breeze?
His hiss is calling my name,
he sits there marking his territory.
He turns his body into a coil
as he stays waiting for his lunch.
He spots a helpless victim,
walking his way.
He waits, patiently
To pounce!
He darts at the scared mouse
And takes it back to his den.
The victim struggles
But after a while,
Gives up.
He swallows the mouse whole
And proudly slithers on.
He finds a shady spot
And here he sets up camp.
He makes himself comfortable
And rattles his tail with pride.
His stomach is full,
his body is rested
And there he stays
All
Night.

Helen Baggott (12)
Tormead School

FRIDAY AFTERNOON

I walk into class, slump into my chair.
Dump my books on the desk
Waiting for the day to end.
The teacher talking about something,
I'm not sure what.
I hear the clock go 'tick, tock, tick . . . '
Suddenly it stops.
'Hooray, the bell!' everyone cries!
Quickly, I gather my heavy books,
Throw them in my bag,
I rush out,
Quicker than you can imagine.
Swinging round the sharp corners,
Down the steep stairs.
The huge doors slamming after me as I glide
Through the long corridors,
Thinking about the weekend.
What a joy it brings!
I hurry out,
The cool, fresh breeze,
Flowing through my face and long hair.
Running quickly in the bright summer sun,
Waiting impatiently,
For my mum!

Lara Norrington (12)
Tormead School

THE BEACH

I sieved the light coloured sand through my fingers,
It felt soft as it slipped gently out of my hand.
I saw a couple running bare-footed along the beach,
They ran towards the splashing blue sea.
The sea was as bright and sparkly as a diamond,
And the frothy waves disappeared around their feet.
I looked around, towels were lying everywhere,
People were asleep or just watching other people swim.
I walked over to the sea, treading on soft sand, and dipped my toes in,
It was biting cold and my toes tingled!
I saw a ring of rock pools and picked up my net,
The algae covered rocks had small pools of water in.
I swished my little net but I did not catch a thing.
I tried again and again but still nothing.
I strolled over lazily to my towel and lay down,
I took out a book and started to read whilst listening to the sounds.
I heard chattering of cheery people, a barking dog,
I heard happy children banging buckets and spades.
After a while I looked around,
Big, beautiful sandcastles had been forming all around me.
I heard the sound of the seagull,
There was a dog chasing a ball.
I took up my book again and thought to myself:
'This is the life,
This is the life, better than all.'

Charlotte Goward (13)
Tormead School

THE LOVE OF A CHILD

A glass of brandy in his hand
Warm and consoling in his leather-bound chair,
Looking out of the window as inside is bland
And on joy outside he has a glassy stare.

Robins chirping on their branch of holly
The festive season enveloped in frost,
The old man lonely, not alone for his folly
But as the one true love of his life is lost.

Another year gone, another to follow
No longer looking forward to tomorrow,
Yearning to meet someone full of life,
For the lonely pain was as sharp as a knife.

The crackling of the fire dwells in the grate
And the old man's heart, devastated by fate,
The love of someone surely would break his sorrow
Daring to hope that loneliness would not follow.

A knock at the door in the crisp afternoon
Waiting for the voice he was anticipating to come soon,
A young, rosy face appeared at the door
And the joy in his heart, he will remember for evermore.

The love of the little child was so warming,
That the poor, old man knew he was still to face many a morning.

Genny Glass (12)
Tormead School

THE TREE HOUSE

Up in the trees
You can see for miles:
Dots that are people walking to and fro,
Cars
Whizzing
By.
People can't see you -
But you see them
Through the leaves and branches
A cosy place
With lots of toys.
You can stay for hours on end
Too high for adults
To invade your privacy.
Birthday presents, Christmas gifts are safe!
Siblings cannot enter
Without ascending the creaking ladder
The windows look onto the pavement
Dogs are scampering past.
Hear the babies gurgling
Up the ladder I scrape my knees
On the sharp corners of the rungs.
You see the old man
Walking past in a grey hat and brown coat
He carries an umbrella come rain or shine.
You can hear the birds.
It is my favourite place to be
On a day like today.

Charlotte Dennis (12)
Tormead School

THE OAK TREE

Hundreds of years,
thousands of leaves have passed by
growing green
then orange, yellow and brown,
the magnificent trunk shoots up and divides into
hundreds of branches and then to the tip of
the tree's leaves.
So many little creatures this oak tree hosts.

Swaying gently in the wind,
the sap glistening in the blinding sun.
We walk, observe and then our life goes on
but the tree stays.

If someone should come and carve their
initials in the trunk, it would forever stay.

If it were not damaged or chopped down.

Hundreds of years gone
to make a desk or a sheet of paper that
would be gone in a few quick months, days
or moments even!

Only the ugly stump left for people to
trip and stumble over. But, in time, it
would reform into its beautiful self with
many acorns to shed.

And so the magnificent cycle would go on.

Sally Bevan (12)
Tormead School

THE PENNY

Something glints on the dusty track,
Gold, silver or is it bronze?
I bend down, pick it up,
Brushing away the dirt,
Carelessly.

A perfect circle,
Moulded boldly,
One in a million,
In striking, raised letters,
'Elizabeth II', 'One penny'.
The coin, forced into the dirt by the tyres of a car,
Passing down the uneven road,
Where the penny lay.
That same portcullis on every single one,
Indistinguishable from the next.

Running my finger over it,
I notice how hard,
How cold it is,
How small and rigid.

This was the penny that bought the sweet
That the child ate.
This was the penny that fell from the pocket of the tramp,
As he walked down this track
Alone.
This was the penny that he left behind
That I picked up.

Robyn Daniel (12)
Tormead School

CHRISTMAS

A warm family gathering,
Creeping downstairs every morning
in the dark and turning on the
Christmas tree lights,
I breathe in the alpine fresh smell of the Christmas tree.
Counting the presents
under the tree
with my name
on.
Visiting relatives that
I see only at Christmas.
Counting the days until Christmas Eve
on your advent calendar.
Visiting the pantomime,
Laying out your stocking on the hearth.
Eating Mum's secret recipe mince pies,
Leaving one sitting on the plate,
Waiting for a burly figure dressed in a crimson-red suit,
To gobble it up on Christmas Eve.
I love the anticipation of lying in bed on Christmas morning,
Waiting until the alarm clock on my bedside table
Starts to beep, telling me
that I can now race downstairs
and open the big sack bulging with . . .
Presents!

Kathryn Maher (13)
Tormead School

WINTER

Frosty windows,
Sprinkled with sugar grains,
Glitter like expensive diamonds.

Ground covered in pure white snow,
As thick as whipped cream,
Seems soft and silky.

Icicles hanging heavily from empty trees,
Like Christmas baubles, shiny and smooth,
Tinkle in a tiny gust of wind.

Winter is as silent as a graveyard,
Pierced by a shrieking owl.

Sunflowers sleep steadily until summer,
Robins roost as the dark night falls.

Long spooky shadows,
Stretching across the ground.

Many stars glimmer,
In the snow-encrusted sky.

A midnight fox,
Prowling the snow.
Eyes shining like topazes,
Bushy tail whooshing as it finds its prey.

The summer has gone,
And winter has arrived.

Krystyna Wilczynski (12)
Tormead School

JOURNEY TO THE PLANETS

10, 9, 8, 7, 6,
Computers buzzing, ready for take-off,
5, 4, 3, 2, 1,
Zero, fire
Planet check list:
Surface, gravity strength, atmosphere,
Pressure, temperature, radiation, wind.
The shining knife cuts into space
The moon, a silver glistening sphere
Swells as the ship approaches
Everyone ready, touchdown
Craters, moon buggies, aliens

This is Mars
An horizon of ice mountains, craters,
Dust storms, deep holes, extinct volcanoes
Letting out an awesome light
Would blind every human eye
Planet of mysteries

Blast off, towards Venus
Pink and glowing,
Picturesque and beautiful,
Dangerously hot
Millions of light years away from the Earth
Orbit once more
Then change direction and head for home.

Kate Griffiths (12)
Tormead School

MIDNIGHT CREATURES

As the moon begins to climb,
a black and white head appears from the ground.
Slowly but surely he comes,
in his fluffy, dark coat.

Scuttling shyly from bush to bush,
nose to the ground as he looks for food.
Then, as day begins to break,
he quietly goes back to his sett.

In fading moonlight, perched in his tree,
the owl gets ready for his nightly trip.
His large brown eyes get set for the dark,
he soars through the air like a fearless dragon.

His sharpened claws waiting to pounce,
on his vulnerable victim.
Those not wary of what's up above,
have their fates already written.

In amongst the tiny shrubs,
beneath the harvest moon,
A small brown twitching figure,
goes darting to and fro.

Eyes so bright and ears a-twitching,
scurrying through fields, nibbling at bits of corn.
Suddenly a noise not far behind,
the mouse, startled, keeps very still.
Waiting, listening, 'til it's safe to move on.

Hannah Lamb (13)
Tormead School

FRENCH EXCHANGE

The ferry stopped,
People rushed from their seats,
All around was mayhem!
The children were spilling out of the ferry onto French ground.

French people, young and old,
Greeted us on the pier,
Friendly faces chatting to each other,
Some crying,
When reunited with their families.

I had to find Sophie, my French exchange,
The search for her was hard and frustrating,
With her photo in my hand,
Trying hard to distinguish her face.
Finally my friend found her.
I saw her,
She was prettier than she was in the photo.

I walked up to her and said 'Hello.'
She seemed pleased to see me for the first time.
Her English was very good,
I was curious so I asked her loads of questions,
This was how I found out how she was really good at English.

We walked off together,
Down to the centre of Paris,
Sophie said it was best to start there.
This was where the fun began!

Zoe Sax (13)
Tormead School

SPLIT

Night fell quickly
Like a curtain ending a play,
The actors left the stage,
To sleep in peace
In the wood.

In the city,
Life was just beginning.
Night watchmen began their rounds,
And the clubs opened
Their doors.

Night creatures awoke -
The timid mouse, the sharp-eyed owl,
One relentlessly hunted by the other.
The badger and the fox smelt the calm
In the wood.

Music blared
From cars full of party-goers.
Dark streets lit by buildings,
Alive with colour and sound
In the city.

Not so long ago,
Both places were the same.
What has man done?
Created a better world or
Made it worse?

Is this how it should be,
In the wood, in the city?

Clare Kissin (13)
Tormead School

CHRISTMAS DAY

Early morning when I opened my eyes,
I pulled the curtains,
Snow was falling.
The trees were covered,
the air was still.
Only footprints of birds to be seen.

I ran down the stairs, excited.
From the fireplace stockings dangled,
but under the tree presents lay!
I heard small voices from upstairs.
I shouted, 'Hurry up! It's Christmas Day!'

As the fire was crackling,
I ripped open my presents,
the paper lay in a heap.
My face full of delight,
I received more than expected.

Time passed and from the kitchen came the aroma
of the turkey sizzling in the oven.
The table was set it was time to eat,
crackers were pulled and the feast began.

It was now 3 o'clock and the laughter had ceased,
we waited patiently for the Queen to speak.
After tears of laughter filled the room,
the game of charades fun for all.

I fell into bed, exhausted,
Christmas Day had come to an end.

Jade Wilkins (13)
Tormead School

ABOVE

They came
Striding along the beach.
Their presence was not known.
It's after dark when they appear,
And daylight is when they are gone.
Only special people see them:
Once!
They come from a place in the sky,
So high up the stars meet at night.
Then taking people from the Earth,
They fly up to the sky and stars.
Taking people, sleeping,
Exchanging their lives.
Little people living on Earth,
Everyday life starts to get hard.
Many wish for one day up there,
None have come back to tell the tale.
People see what they wish to see,
It's what they make in their dreams.

Charlotte Garthwaite (13)
Tormead School

FRIENDS

F riends are like fairytales sent from above
R evolving and turning
I   n bubbles of kindness and
E verlasting happiness. Friends
N ever forget each other and remember each other
D ay after day. Friends
S tay friends forever.

Georgia Knight (11)
Tormead School

REFLECTION

Sunlight shining through leaves creates dancing shadows
Small droplets of dew carpet the grass
Carefree clouds hitch a lift on the wind
Gradually our side of the world is awakening

A light breeze skipping, running like a young child at play
I shiver but not from any cold
The stillness of the early morning
Silent as a pool of unrippling water

Pushing thoughts of the day ahead, out of my mind
Concentrating only on this moment
I remember words spoken years ago
Laughing at life, I wait for the moment to end

I can see a small movement in the house behind me
My parents are no longer asleep
Shouting voices reach me even here
I smile softly and walk back into the mayhem.

Miranda Voke (13)
Tormead School

WINTER

A blanket of cold white snow,
Covering rooftops as it goes,
Tall green pines sprinkled with white,
Like cake icing, as across it blows.

Children in gloves, scarves, woolly hats,
Shrieks of delight, making snowmen and snowballs,
The puff of misty breath as mothers' chat
The crunch of snow under their heavy footfalls.

A little house, all cosy and warm,
A blazing fire, the curtains drawn,
A steaming pot of piping hot tea,
A plate of buttered crumpets,
Waiting for me.

Kaylee Lemieux (12)
Tormead School

THE RAINBOW

When the rain begins to fall
It trickles down a dusty wall.
It carries on along the street
And gently splashes people's feet.

Everywhere is damp and wet
An umbrella you must get.
Swish, swash, splish, splash
Can't talk now, got to dash.

When the sun is shining bright
The water will reflect the light.
If it does, what will appear
But a rainbow bright and clear.

Pink, violet, blue and green
So many colours to be seen.
There is a story to be told
That at the end, a pot of gold.

The gold has not been found by children
Hidden in a big black cauldron.
Is this because there is no end
To the beautifully coloured rainbow bend?

Chloe Chambers (13)
Tormead School

REMEMBERING

Staring out across the wet,
dull street,
Remembering.

Touching her wedding ring,
a tear runs down her old,
withered cheek,
Crying.

She remembers running along the river,
her husband holding her hand,
Smiling.

Her long blonde hair is flowing behind her,
she swings her arms around him,
as they walk together,
her young face,
Laughing.

Walking away,
holding hands,
happy and hopeful,
as they fade into the distance,
Loving.

The old lady clutches her tissue,
she sniffs and looks down,
times have changed,
there's no one left,
as her tears fall to the ground,
Mourning.

Emma Johnson (13)
Tormead School

FIRE

Crimson and yellow flames
Gently licked the maple fireplace walls.
While erratic crackling
Made the capacious cat scowl.

Cosy smells filled the room,
A small burning aroma
Overcame the wooden chamber,
Another log was tossed upon the fire.

'Lovely fire' the son said softly,
His father smiled proudly
Lying relaxed in his cracked leather chair.
'Thank you' in his deep comforting voice.

They sat silently in the room,
One reading yesterday's paper,
The other focusing on the fire
While the windchimes whistled in the wind.

Hot flames overcame the room,
With its newly polished pine walls
And recently dusted bookcases
Storing books of pirates' tales and pantomimes.

Open windows slammed shut,
Fires died in brisk breezes.
Darkness and cold fell over the room.
Silence, as the men rose uncomfortably.
'Shame about the fire' said the son.
'Never mind' said the father.

Lucy McGauran (13)
Tormead School

FIVE HOURS OF ANTICIPATION

The room full of excitement and anticipation.
Secrets of many months revealed,
There hung the beautiful, crisp, white dress,
The detailed lace exquisite.

Beside were our bridesmaids' dresses,
The cream of lilies,
The blue of cornflowers.
There, five pairs of cream ballet slippers,
Five delicate silver chains placed on the table
Each sparkling in the sun.

I slipped on my silky tights,
Stepped into my fairytale gown.
My hair was exotically twisted back,
I felt like a ballerina, a real ballerina.

A wink and a smile from the bride's father,
We turned to perform for the camera.
The stiff taffeta loosened by the breeze,
The flowers left a sweet aroma.

I walked into the white car.
The engine began, we were off,
Following the glamorous bride.
People passing gazed at us,
I felt famous!

My butterflies began to fly frantically.
The doors opened, the organ began.
My head held high, I walked up the aisle.

Helen Derbyshire (13)
Tormead School

THE WANDERER

Snow falling
From leaden clouds
Blurring the light
In the descending gloom.

Night drawing in.
Cold increasing.
Wind whistling eerily
Like a hundred lost souls.

A silhouette came into view
Trudging over the hills
With thin, ragged clothes
Pulled tight against the chill.

Mumbling quietly
He staggered through the drifting snow
Up hill and down dale
No path or road to follow.

Storm became blizzard.
He stopped.
Confused and lost,
Then ran blindly.

He called out
But his voice was lost
In the raging blast.
He battled on desperately.

He tripped and stumbled
Snow giving way
Above a hidden chasm
Soon to be his icy tomb.

Emily Grosvenor Taylor (13)
Tormead School

THE STORM

Hills went rolling into the blue.
The sky an array of most glorious hues.
Waves came lapping up onto the beach,
Chasing each other right to my feet.

Chilling my nose as I sniffed the air,
A salty sea breeze ruffled my hair.
The sky turned grey, the sun was gone.
I suddenly realized I was all alone.

Far out at sea, a grey cloud appearing,
Coming over the horizon, ever nearing.
As it came closer still, the waves white and foaming.
The calm blue seas now raging black waters.

I jumped up to leave; rain began to pour,
It fell down in sheets, I could see no more.
The tide coming up, what could I do?
Nowhere to go, no way through.

Suddenly standing knee-deep in water,
The cold ran through me like electricity.
A white-tipped wave was rolling towards me
I screamed for help, my mouth filled with sea water.
I fell choking into the swirling, dangerous darkness.

As I slowly drifted back to consciousness,
I felt the warm sun shining down on me.
I heard the seagulls cawing up overhead.
I smelt the bracing sea air, awaking my senses.
As I opened my eyes I saw the beach,
Calm and deserted as it had been,
Before the storm.

Roxane Gergaud (13)
Tormead School

RAIN

Looking outside,
Seeing it hitting the window,
Droplets sliding slowly down,
Constant tappings on the roof
Like a drummer pounding mercilessly
on my brain.
Dull green trees and cold grey skies,
How bleak and barren.

Sitting inside, watching outside,
Warm glows all around.
Hoping for blue skies and sun,
Knowing that will not happen
We sit and stare.
Nothing to do and nothing to say,
What a day.

Heavier and heavier, as time passes by,
Lashing at the window,
From slowly sliding
To covering the glass like a vertical carpet.
Will it rain for eternity,
Never to end?

Suddenly things dramatically changed,
Clouds began to drift apart
Letting rays of light beam through.
Colours came back, bringing life to everything.
I think I preferred the rain.

Zehra Zaidi (13)
Tormead School

ALL ALONE

The rain was drumming on the window,
As I got up I knew something was wrong.
Downstairs I saw it:
A mess!

Mum and Dad were not in bed,
The bed had not been slept in.
Downstairs again,
I looked around.
The house was still.
I called for Mum,
I called for Dad,
No one answered.

I searched every room,
Then I went into the kitchen
Where I heard a whimpering.
I'd forgotten all about Sarah our dog.
I climbed over the mess and opened the door,
Sarah bounded out,
She was following a scent.

Sarah wanted to go down into the cellar.
Down the stairs to the cellar,
I could hear my heart pounding through the darkness.
'Mum, Dad?' I whispered.
I slumped onto the floor,
Tears welled up in my eyes.
'Kate?' croaked a voice from the darkness.

Bethany Baker (13)
Tormead School

THE EXCITEMENT OF HOCKEY MATCHES

Excitement building at the start,
Breathing getting faster.
Ball passed one to another.

The crack of a ball on a stick,
The smell of freshly cut grass.
The running in the rain.
Determination in the air.

Players running up and down with
The squelching mud beneath their feet.
Faces burning with heat,
Supporters shouting 'Win this time!'

At last the half-time whistle blows,
Relief comes over.
Breathing quickly, drinking fast,
Waiting for the second half.

Yet another whistle blows,
They are ready to score.
As they come onto the pitch
The crowd cheers.

Back in focus, back in the mood.
Always missing the goal.
They tried but could not score
That triumphant goal.

Did they ever score a goal?
Yes, with only minutes to go
To that final whistle.

Jocelyn Parminter (13)
Tormead School

THE OUTSIDER

Standing out in the crowd,
Standing all alone.
Feeling lonely and depressed
Thinking that something is wrong with you,
But it is not you, it's them.

In everyone's secrets,
Being laughed at.
Sometimes trying to be like them,
But never succeeding
Always looking worse.

Never telling anyone,
Keeping it to yourself.
Keeping the tears inside,
Remembering what happened before
Coming out black and blue.

Always called names,
Never asked to go out.
Never asked to be in their group,
Wanting to know what is wrong with you
What's the matter?

Being scared,
No friends, no happiness.
Life is unhappy going downhill,
Everything is affected
Marks go down.

All you want is to be dead?

Megan Thomas (13)
Tormead School

THE COLOURS OF SUMMER

The colours of summer can be
Green for grass
And pink for flowers
Golden as the sun in the sky
But summer is really a rainbow of colours.

Summer is hot, as hot as the barbecue
Summer is cool, as cool as ice lollies
Summer is quiet with only birds singing
Summer is loud when aeroplanes zoom over
Summer is different with all these senses.

Summer is full of exciting things
Barbecues and outdoor parties
Holidays and fishing trips
Late nights and late starts
Summer is wonderful with all these activities.

Summer is relaxing
When lazing by the poolside
Summer is tiring
When hiking up steep hills
Summer is fun with all of these.

The colours of summer can be
Green for grass
And pink for flowers
Golden as the sun in the sky
But summer is really a rainbow.

Emily Prior (12)
Tormead School

THE BAZAAR OF ASWAN

Sun beats down
on buyers' faces
amidst the scene of reds,
greens, blues and yellows,
of stalls and traders,
at the Bazaar
of Aswan.

Anything you wish to buy,
spices, silks, scarves, sarongs,
will be found at the 'very best price'
in amongst the stalls
at the Bazaar
of Aswan.

Traders cry out
'See the treasure I have
of the highest quality'
as they display beautiful bejewelled boxes
at the Bazaar
of Aswan.

Bright galabeas flutter
as flowers in a tree
and rhinestones glint
to reflect mini-worlds
exactly the same as
the Bazaar
of Aswan.

These things combined
make a different realm
far from the hassled world,
a realm of colours and laughter
at the Bazaar
of Aswan.

Emily Bell (14)
Tormead School

THE RACE

I fly off the blocks and the water chills my skin,
my ears are closed to the racket I could hear
before I dived in.
At 100m I've just finished the fly,
it feels like an hour has gone by.
It's a tie between me and the girl in the next lane,
I keep working, going through all the pain.
I know I can win and win I will,
even though my legs are already starting to kill.
I hear my coach scream,
I really don't want to let down my team.
Stroke, stroke, stroke, breath, my rhythm doesn't stop,
but around 300m I feel I want to drop.
My free was good,
if only I could . . .
Yes! I hear the shouts and cheers from the side,
a sensation runs through my body of pride.
I had won,
now to get out, I felt as if my body weighed a ton.
As I stood in first place,
I just remembered my exciting and tiring race!

Vicky Whitehorn (13)
Tormead School

I Wonder What It Would Be Like To Drink Sunshine?

I think
a sunshine drink
is yellow
and very mellow.

Its taste
you'd never waste,
for it would
be so good.

In winter it would warm you up
and make you happy and gay.
You'd never feel cold, the heat would always
keep the chill away.

Its bouquet
they would say
is fresher
than spring weather.

So fizzy
you'd be dizzy
with bubbles
that melt your troubles.

So there you have it a sunshine drink
is the healthiest thing to date,
so somebody somewhere invent some now
before it is too late.

Emma Butterworth (12)
Tormead School

PUDDLES

In the night, through the day,
plipping, plopping, splashing,
running, puddles forming.

Over the ground, the
grass, the path, flowing,
growing, getting bigger.

Someone sees us,
betrays us, doesn't stop us.
The tarmac getting blacker.

Soaking arms stretch,
floating leafy boats.
The earth overflowing with water.

Even the roofs,
our droplets and puddles
dripping through ceilings.

We shoulder through holes,
widening crannies,
washing the soil away.

We take and we break,
but no hurt is intended
to those beneath our fall.

Sometimes we're loud,
raucous, a drumming, but
then we turn quiet and small.

Run to the sea,
return to the sky.
Then we are puddles again.

Tabitha Hutton (15)
Tormead School

A SPARKLING DREAM

My mother one day did awaken me,
Told me to look out the window and what did I see?
There before me everything sparkled and gleamed.
It was magic and glittery.
The treetops beamed.
Icing was spread all over the grass,
The lake looked like a sheet of glass.
The trees were covered from head to toe
With wonderful magical glistening snow.
I rushed outside in my wellington boots,
As I crunched in the snow I tripped on tree roots.
My feet got cold, but I did not care,
I knew this was God's work, his decorations spare.
My mother called me . . . I did not listen.
I had to watch this world before me glisten.

Carly Smith (12)
Tormead School

WINTER

The days are getting shorter
And the evenings getting dark,
No more evening cycle rides,
Or football in the park.

The brilliant green leaves on the trees
Are turning brown and red,
The squirrels and the hedgehogs
Will soon curl up in bed.

The wind is whistling all around
And all the trees are swaying,
The brown leaves flutter to the ground,
Out there they are not staying.

And when I'm lying in my bed,
Listening to the rain,
I snuggle down between the sheets
And dream of spring again.

Lucy Anwyl (13)
Tormead School

AT A FOOTBALL GAME!

Fresh cut grass as green as a rose stem,
Contrasting white lines, crisp and clear.
Thousands of seats filling up with red and blue.

Feet start stomping like a team of schoolboys,
And cheers gather into steady rhythms.
A thud of a header and a whack of a hard kick.

The smell of sweat off the twenty-two players,
Or the greasy stench of a juicy hamburger.
I sniff the staleness of old matches through my scarf.

I taste warm comfort through my hot chocolate,
And as I bite into my hamburger, the warmth hurts my teeth.
Or the contrasting temperature of a cold coke.

The cold bites at my fingers,
I lose the feeling in my toes.
All my cold is forgotten when my team scores that first goal!

Claudia Condon (14)
Tormead School

THE SENSES

A dark mist enveloped the loch
in the eerie silence,
I listened: the water advanced up the pebbles,
I listened: the water retreated
to the depths of the black water.

I watched the pebbles shine like jewels
and the clouds roll over the mountain tops,
skimming the snow as they passed.
I watched the trees stand perfectly still,
void of any life.

I felt the cool wind seep through my body,
it froze my face and breath,
I felt the waves beneath my feet,
leaving them cold and icy.

I tasted the salt that splashed my face,
stinging my eyes and burning my lips,
I smelt the seaweed that lay all around me
barely living,
the frosty air sharply froze my nose as I inhaled.

A dark mist enveloped the loch
in the eerie silence,
I listened, I watched, I felt, I tasted, I smelt
everything around me
leaving my senses stunned and numb.

Jenna Crombie (14)
Tormead School

FEAR

Terrified, shaking, cold sweat dripping down his face:
Tears of fear,
Tears of despair,
Tears of rage,
There he stood, still - everything silent.
Suddenly, footsteps running across the field,
The footsteps of his companions.
Crusting cannons pierced his ears,
Cries of young men as their lives lay on this battlefield.
Cries, agonies, never seeming to stop.
Suddenly, everything is quiet again as the last man stumbles.
He looks: all he sees is a pall of smoke, a pool of blood,
                                        a pool of tears.
All alone he crouches, head down,
Shaking like a leaf in the wind.
All the life that was once around him - gone,
The hope that was once around him - gone.
Reluctantly, he rises - takes one last look at the surroundings,
Takes one big step into the field,
Takes one final run to the beat of his heart,
Faster and faster until the excruciating cannon strikes again.
There he lies, united with his companions once again.

Lindsey Charlton (14)
Tormead School

REQUIEM FOR A FISH

Two swimming around the tank.
Two playing among the rocks,
The plastic weeds.

Given as a sixth birthday present -
One of a pair.
From a friend, now nearly forgotten,
Distant - we never kept in touch.

Needle, she died, and Thread she left.
Once named Fishy and Belinda;
Lucinda and Belinda;
Belinda and Belinda;
Needle and Thread.

Now just Thread.

A pet throughout my childhood years.
As they draw to a close, so too did she.
Things change.

Two swam around the tank.
Two played among the rocks,
The plastic weeds.

Part of a pair.
Now just one.

One swims around the tank.
One plays among the rocks,
The plastic weeds.

A pair no more.
One's gone; left the
Other goldfish alone,
As one.

Fiona Doyle (14)
Tormead School

WHO?

Who is He and what does He look like?
Blond or brunette,
Fat or thin,
Tall or short.
What is His name?
No one knows Him,
So no once can really answer any of these questions.
So why do we search for the answers?
We all talk to Him,
At least once in our lives.
A man people trust unconditionally,
A man people love unconditionally.
Why do we trust Him?
Why do we love Him?
Because deep down in our hearts we all believe He is there
and listening.
Creating war in Kosovo, Sarejevo and Northern Ireland
Kills some, and scars other people for life.
Poverty-stricken and homeless people still keep on believing in Him.
He may be the only person in their lives who loves them,
So why would He create these wars, why would He create this poverty?
He is indestructible, imperishable and immortal.
He takes care of us and listens when no one else will.
We trust and love Him and somewhere inside us we all believe.
He creates war and poverty for reasons no one understands.
He has the almighty power to do this.

He is God.

Pippa Kober (14)
Tormead School

BEST FRIENDS

Friends are vital!
Always there for you
Eager to listen
Protective an honest
They are what you need
Portraying love
Unique and special
Providing confidence every day
Giggling and laughing
Shopping every weekend
They will always be there
A part of your life
Have something to say
Dependant on them
Providing the best of advice
Always a helping hand
Discussing memories
Sharing all with them
Comforting you
Never missing a remarkable day
Always welcoming you
Including you in conversation
Fantastic personalities
Always keep you busy
Sharing the joys of life
They are your finest friends!

Carlyn van Rensburg (14)
Tormead School

AFRICA

From a hidden depth beneath the world
A crown of light emerges.
Slowly, gradually, but determined to rise,
Crimson sunlight floods the vast savannahs.

Intriguing species roam the plains,
Their silhouettes dissolving into oblivion.
Throbbing heat penetrates down,
Another day is evolving.

Maasai tribes in burgundy robes
Walk amongst their inherited lands,
Dance and laugh beneath the clouds
And celebrate their lives together.

The atmosphere begins to cool
As slender clouds move on by
The game relaxing, though still alert
Keep watch for stalking predators.

The King, the beast, the regal lion
Strides and views his golden kingdom.
Close behind him, his loyal pride
Venture in their wild territory.

Dusk approaches, day starts to fade
Breezes whirl, then disappear.
The radiant sun descends from his throne
And the moon succeeds his vital role.

A black sky, studded with pearls
Looks down upon the quiet Earth,
Although no sound enters the air,
The circle of life lives on.

Annika Mantle (14)
Tormead School

NOTHING TO SAY

I can't understand why your life is so far from the truth,
Your congress and accomplishments are maximised,
While mine are frowned upon.
To me, your life is like a new, false language
That I just can't understand,
Maybe I didn't listen to you,
But I don't speak for the sake of speaking,
I speak from my heart,
And all my words reveal me,
That's why I have nothing to say to you.

It seems amusing to me that you consider yourself great,
So beautiful, so precious and outstanding.
The suffering you feel from me is all due to your changed worth
And when the smoke gets in your eyes,
You trust me,
Yet I denounce you because I can't stand to see you
Disrespect yourself
To disrespect me.
You always told me to give you my hand
And you'd make me understand,
But that was so far from the truth,
That's why I have nothing to say to you.

Catriona Forrest (15)
Tormead School

BENEATH THE SKY

The burning sphere of dazzling gold
Floating far out on the horizon
Glistens in the stained blue sky.
All alone I sit and wait an endless
Pause of time.

The faintest sound of delicate feet
Winding their way along the jetty,
Still I sit staring dreamily,
Eyes fixed upon the aqua glass
Lying beneath my feet.

The sun does dance no more,
But the starlit sky which glistens
With jewels encircles the glowing moon.
A significant sign for a special night,
Still I sit and dream.

The sun gone out, the cold creeps in,
Trees whispering far across the lake.
Chilling visions fill my head.
A hand! A hand? A face! A beautiful face,
Starry eyes, hair of silk, the face
unique and warming.

The sheer relief, complete security
Fills the unending void.
Hand in hand we depart from the lake,
Where I will sit alone no longer.

Elizabeth Webb (14)
Tormead School

FOUR SEASONS

Bright sunlight shines
On the shimmering snow.
Cold breezes shiver in and out of bare trees.
Everything is quiet,
Everything is still.

Dew covered grass
Stands tall to attention.
Newborn lambs dance and frolic.
Everything is calm,
Everything is fresh.

The sights, smells and sounds of happiness
Are in the air.
A young girl laughs, loving such a pleasant day.
Everything is jolly.
Everything is happy.

All around colour floats
And falls to the ground.
The sun retires, takes a well-earned rest.
Everything is colourful, but
Everything is dull.

It is amazing how one place
Can change just in one year.
Winter, spring, summer, autumn,
Each brings their own thrills.
Everything can change and
Everything will.

Jenny Prideaux (15)
Tormead School

You May Not Hear Me

You may not hear me in the morning rush,
Or in the silent evening hush.
You may not see me in your sleep,
On mountains high or oceans deep.
You may not touch me when you cry,
Or when your tears are running dry.
Although I am gone, I am still here.
I will not leave you, do not fear.
I am the birds that fly so high,
I am the thousand stars in the sky.
I am the sun that burns so bright,
I am the early morning light.
I am soft church bells that ring,
I am the autumn breezes that sing.
I am the strong, cool winds that blow,
I am the sunflowers of golden yellow.
When you feel the grass beneath your feet,
Think of where we used to meet.
When you feel the sun warm your face,
Think of that special place.
Remember where we used to lie,
Remember all the passers-by.
Although we cannot relive those days,
I will be with you, now and always.

Carla Watchman (15)
Tormead School

THE CIRCLE OF LIFE

A bird flies into a tree.
The cheetah opens his eyes,
Yawns, then stretches.

His stomach rumbles
And he gets to his feet.
A mouse scuttles under the ground.

He prowls around, sniffing the air,
A herd of deer grazes peacefully nearby.
With his nose up high, ears pricked forward, he slowly
Walks in their direction.

Lying under the cover of a tree, he looks towards them,
Impatiently pawing the ground
As he waits for the right moment to attack.

In his pre-pouncing posture, he breathes heavily
Then jumps up and majestically sprints covering a metre
                              with each bound,
Towards the deer.

A smaller deer falls behind, the cheetah is almost at his tail.
Using his last bit of energy, he pounces,
And kills him in one bite.

Hovering protectively over his meal
He lies there, tongue lolling out to the side to recover,
Then drags his meal back to his den.

In a matter of minutes, he finishes his food,
Then after licking himself proudly at his catch, he yawns
And resting his head on his paws, falls back to sleep.

Christina Davis (14)
Tormead School

CRYING FOR FOOD

Children, lying in shacks,
tears running down their narrow faces as they cry for food.
As they labour in the fields in the hot summer sun,
I can see their need for water,
but the water they are forced to walk miles for every day is nothing
more
than liquid mud.
The crops are dying and starvation is great as children cry for food.
They play in the mud to amuse themselves,
for there is no school to attend and no toys to play with.
The rags they wear show their skeleton bodies as they beg their
mothers for food:
'What's for dinner tonight, Mummy?' I hear one small and slender
girl inquire,
'Nothing tonight, darling' I hear her mother reply.
'Daddy will have some food for us tomorrow, I promise.'
I can see the worried look on her face as she turns to her husband,
Afraid of what tomorrow will bring.
Three words spring into mind as I watch the village struggling
to survive:
Malnourishment, starvation and poverty.
I carry on walking through the sunlit village, deep in thought
and wondering what I will see next.

Marie Szachniewicz (14)
Tormead School

THE STORM

The whispering winds,
The clouds that form,
The beating rain that falls.
Listen as they try to warn,
Give into the strength of the storm.

The clattering doors,
The straining trees,
The gnashing jaws that stir the seas.
Just watch them as they try to warn,
Give into the strength of the storm.

The spirited storm,
The death of life,
The final blow to human strife,
So helpless now, just feel them warn,
Give into the strength of the storm.

It rages on,
The monstrous black,
The heartless beast that swallows all.
So ask your neighbour and your Lord,
Why did you send this storm?

The murderous wars,
The endless disease,
The hazards of land and sea.
We once were strong, but now are weak,
We'll give into the strength of the storm.

Abi Welsh (14)
Tormead School

RAIN

Cold drops of moisture fall upon my neck,
I look up.
I see the rain clouds beginning to break.
The school bell rings,
A sudden shrill,
Children march into school.
Now we're trapped inside,
'Kept safe and dry,'
Then,
A gentle sound of drips,
I look up
To see a leak,
The rain slowly dripping through,
We could not be kept apart for long.
It was back,
Oh what a sight,
To see it raining inside, as well as out.
We jumped for joy and began to shout.
The bell rang,
It was class time,
Science, what a bore.
I searched for signs of leaks
But nothing,
All was well sealed.
I sat beside the window where
I longingly looked outside with despair,
The rain had gone,
The sun was out,
A rainbow filled the sky with colour,
Only bringing memories of what had been.

Lottie Tollman (14)
Tormead School

THAT PERSON STANDING NEXT TO ME

Who is he?
Who is she?
What is he doing?
What is she doing?
Why oh why don't I know the answers?

What has he brought?
What has she bought?
What is he thinking?
What is she drinking?
Why oh why don't I know the answers?

I know I'm only human,
Nothing special, no one strange,
I'm in exactly the same position as
That person standing next to me.

Then why can't I just accept this,
Look at someone, then look away.
I suppose I want to know everyone, just like
That person standing next to me.

I'm insecure and quiet,
I'd never look someone in the eye, or go and ask their name,
I need to hold my head up high, just like
That person standing next to me.

Who is that person standing next to me?
A fashion victim? A great entrepreneur?

No!

She has wit, she has style,
She is beautiful, she is intelligent,
Because in my dreams, I am
That person standing next to me.

Bryony Whittaker (15)
Tormead School

IS IT WORTH IT?

Slowly wandering down the beach,
so lost in thought
she hardly hears the sound of the powerful waves
crashing onto the shore.
The feeling of warm tears
steadily falling down her pale face
is her only comfort,
and yet is causing her so much pain.
Countless questions left to be asked,
but will any be answered?
Never again shall she be reassured by his presence,
for his presence never again shall be.
Knowing that she is not alone
makes her feel even more so,
as no one could ever feel the same way.
The well-meant questions of concern
are what is tearing her apart.
Standing at the edge of a massive cliff,
gazing out over the great ocean,
lost.
Should she do it?
Is it worth it?

Thea Zevenbergen (14)
Tormead School

SCHOOL

Twenty 'intellectual' teenagers in a shabby classroom,
Listening 'intently' to the fascinating teacher.
Seconds, minutes, hours pass, feeling like a lifetime.
'Why? What? I don't understand, what's this got to do with
                                    the rest of our lives?'
Questions drone through the room.

I look around studying friends' faces,
Every one in a world of their own,
Different thoughts racing through their minds.
Every class has a couple,
The ones who listen, take in and understand,
Every one else relies on last minute cramming.

I turn to the teacher,
To some, a sad, pathetic figure prattling on about useless facts,
                                    names and dates,
I take a deeper more realistic outlook.
She wanders throughout the room,
Frantically trying to make us understand, pass our exams.
She could just walk out, I would.

She's trying so hard yet we are just scribbling notes,
Passing them under our desks,
Our heads in our hands,
Our eyes glazed over desperately trying to prevent them from closing.
In her mid-sentence, the bell rings,
Jumping up, packing our bags as quickly as possible,
We run out of the door,
Still the poor teacher stands at the front of the room, ending her
                                    sentence alone.

Sally-Anne Davies (14)
Tormead School

MEMORIES HURT

There he sat alive as can be,
With his old smile,
And white hair like wire,
I remember it clearly.

I ran in and jumped on his lap,
I nearly squashed the cat,
He hugged me, he said he loved me,
I remember it clearly.

He built our house,
Saw him on the roof,
Where shall this tile go Bec?
I remember it clearly.

I remember the day Dad flew off,
He looked pale and sad,
I was only three, I was scared,
I remember it clearly.

It was my fourth birthday party,
Dad phoned,
It wasn't to wish us happy birthday,
I remember it clearly.

Mum looked shocked and pale,
She didn't know what to tell us,
She just said that Oupa had gone.
I remember him clearly.

Becky Hofmeyr (13)
Tormead School

Door

Everybody knows I'm here,
I'm swung this way and that,
I stand up straight and wait,
I often gaze longingly out of the window
In hope of someone coming to rescue me,
Then finally someone is home,
She enters the empty room, slamming me behind her.

As she gazes out of the window,
I stand there watching her tear-strewn face,
My bright white paint gleaming in the summer sun.

As the night falls, I start to sway this way and that,
I'm afraid of the dark . . .
But wait!
I hear a sound,
I feel my shiny brass handle being turned.
Who can it be?
It is too dark to see,
They leave without a sound.
Now I long for morning, the bright crisp morning.
How I long for you.

Abi Butterworth (13)
Tormead School

The Kitchen Clock

I am blue, shaped like a plate,
Small and circular.
My hands tick round and round;
I run on a battery, nothing stopping me,
Put there for a purpose,
To show the time of day -
Late or early, dark or light.

I am never cruel, yet always truthful,
Surveying the comings and goings,
Listening to the household noises,
In a quick, thoughtful way.

Joanna Willcox (13)
Tormead School

UNDERWATER

A calm, harmonic place to be,
Is under the surface of the superior blue, silk sheet.
The harlequin of graceful sea creatures,
The colours of peace and comfort,
So subtle and exquisite.

You can hear the haunting sounds
Which belong to the unknown,
The sparkling jewels, while blinding you,
Are whispering softly with angelic voices.
It's all music to my ears, it's a relief to my mind.

How can such an admirable setting
Make me taste fear?
I fear the completeness in this world,
It could never all be virtuous, surrounding me
Are the awaiting eyes of strangers.

Some are drooling with the malicious hunger,
others seem nauseatingly innocent, yet encouraging,
But I just can't trust what I don't comprehend.
I can't live in a world which plays with my mind.
The world above isn't perfect, but it seems comfortable.

Rosanna Flynn (14)
Tormead School

THE BALLOON RIDE

Flying towards the fluffy, white clouds,
Into the clear, blue sky
Away from the chaos into the calm,
As we rose from the quilted land.

Our beautiful balloon blew in the breeze
As peacefully as a dove,
All the people down below
Were staring up above.

Houses turned into matchboxes
Which huddled along black lace.
Cars turned into tiny moving shapes
And trees into spots of green.

The giant flame appeared again
As the gas was lit,
The gas which kept our basket high,
Above busy life below.

Slowly, softly, our balloon began to fall,
Back towards the noise,
The steady sound of cars moving
And the beep of a horn.

Back from the calm into the chaos,
Back to our daily lives,
Back from the calm into the chaos,
Back to our busy lives.
Back from the calm into the chaos.

Emily Wilson (14)
Tormead School

AFRICA

Tourists go to Africa,
Admire the beautiful land, wild creatures.
They're blind to the poor country,
Blind to the desperate children.

Masai sell their souvenirs to tourists,
Tourists are oblivious that tribes-people have walked,
Walked two days in heat and dust to sell their goods.
Tourists then only buy a small African necklace,
Leaving the tribe to walk home again, with despair.

A pen will help towards their children's education,
Here, it would be a small item.
A small item to slip down the side of a sofa,
Why do we allow this cruelty?

The lowest-class job you could get here
Would be the highest-class in Africa.
Africans are grateful for everything.
Maybe we should learn from them,
Instead of them learning from us.

Humans are unaware of others in need
And even crying, empty hands
Are not held or comforted
But ignored as you pass them by.

It is like they are merely a painting on the wall,
To be looked at but to be left alone.

Lisette Voûte (14)
Tormead School

AWAY FROM REALITY

As I open my eyes to this wonderful world,
This incredible place has to be told.
Lying there, listening and watching as I look around,
Surrounding the island, an ocean of mysteries.

The peaceful sound of waves ebbing and flowing,
The children building sandcastles and playing.

White skin turning golden brown,
Coins in the sand ready to be found.

The hot sun spreads its rays over the island,
Pleasing everyone with its heat.

The smell of sun cream covering my body
joins that of the salty, sea air.

As I reach out to touch the golden sand,
The grains slide slowly through my fingers.

Suddenly I remember, tomorrow I'll be home,
Enjoying the last few moments away from reality.

Katherine Mollart (13)
Tormead School

I'M A TOOTHBRUSH

I'm a toothbrush.
I work hard morning, noon and night,
My bristles are long and lush,
Coloured black and white.

I brush off the plaque
And get rid of the dirt,
I take all the flack
When the nerves start to hurt.

'This tooth really hurts,
It has hundreds of holes,
That brush didn't work,
It's missed its goal.'

So here I am
In the rubbish bin,
He took me out
And put another toothbrush in.

Amy Catten (13)
Tormead School

THE SOFA

Sometimes I am a seat,
Sometimes I am a bed,
Sometimes I am a castle,
Sometimes I am a boat, bright red.

I feel the weight of many,
I feel soft to them.
I am a magic potion,
For all types of men.

A fiery battle,
With me as the weapon.
Being hurled around like a rattle,
Or being their strong protection.

In the room I see the normal,
A table, an armchair and a TV.
Sometimes I must be smart and formal,
Other times, I can be plain old me!

Felicity Boyle (13)
Tormead School

An Ode To The Unknown Soldier

The haunted sound
Of soldiers crying
From the pain of wounds,
The loss of pride.

The deafening rain
Pelting down on our helmets,
As we slide
Through the mud stream of death.

Lying in the filthy trenches
Our hearts beating boldly,
We must be courageous
For our families and fellow soldiers.

Through the shooting of guns,
The only sound
Is the deep breathing
Of the soldier close by.

A brief interval,
Then the guns start again.
We try to rest,
But there is little chance.

All of a sudden
Comes the command to go.
This is it,
Our turn to move.

Up over the trench
To bare ourselves to the enemy.
The soldier to my right
Breathes no more.

Amelia Whiston-Dew (13)
Tormead School

DISASTER STRIKES!

The earth bumping under my feet,
Sirens sounding noisily,
People rushing about,
Screaming!
Scared!
Thoughts going through my head.
Fear of what will happen,
What shall I do?
Help!
Help!
No one to listen.

An aftershock appears,
I fall to the ground,
Scared!
Pain rushing through my leg!
Everything shaking
Shivering.
Crash,
A glass fell to the ground,
I am in fear of death,
'Mum, Mummy'
I hear the children cry.
Stop!
Stop!
Please help me.
Disaster strikes!

Emily Prideaux (13)
Tormead School

ALL ALONE

Grey clouds loomed in the distance,
Thunder rumbled far away.
Waves rolled and crashed on the shore,
Pounding the beach with a mighty roar.
The beach was deserted.

Rain pelted down on my face,
The wind was as fierce as an angry bull.
The piercing cry of a seagull cut through the darkness.
The fog-horn of a passing boat dinned through my ears,
The beach was deserted.

The flash of the light-house beamed through the mist,
Ships' masts clinked and clanked,
The sea grass in the dunes waved and whispered,
Clouds gathered and darkened.
The beach was deserted.

I wandered up the lonely beach,
Looking at every sight,
Listening to every sound.
I felt the strong wind whip my hair.
The beach was deserted.

The sky was beginning to become overcast,
The silhouette of the moon came slowly into view.
I watched the cruel grey waves as they rolled towards me
As I stood on that cold and windy shore all alone.
The beach was deserted.

Charlotte Robertson (13)
Tormead School

THE SHOE

People walk all over me,
As if they have more authority,
Little do they know
I control them.

I am in a partnership,
I like it that way.
I know I am not alone
And I only do half the work.

We pass expensive Italian shoes,
Made of the best leather,
But we just sneer,
As we know we are much more dependable.

Trainers are the best breed,
We are much more faithful.
Size fives are perfect,
Not too big, not too small.

You can't trust these Italians,
They think they're too good for the best of feet,
Unlike us,
Dependable shoes.

Jyoti Sekhawat (13)
Tormead School

WINTERTIME

Winter - give a hearty cheer,
For Christmas Day will soon be here.
There is such a lot to do,
Pantomimes and circus too.

Soon it will start to snow,
We will leave footprints as we go.
We make snowballs and a slide,
Take the sledge and have a ride.

I'll run downstairs on Christmas morn,
When Jesus Christ was once born.
Parties, treats so many things,
Make the fun the season brings.

At Christmas time we all have a treat,
All the presents wrapped so neat.
All the Christmas lights are glowing,
And the wind is wildly blowing.

After all that Christmas dinner,
We all wish we were a little thinner.
For dessert I made a cake
Which took a long time to bake.

My Christmas cake is delicious,
It was extremely nutritious.
It's going to be a big surprise
For my family, I hear their cries.

Our Christmas tree is very white,
With all the lights it looks so bright.
With carols, paper chains and toys
Brings the time for many joys.

Laura Hay (13)
Tormead School

THE LOYALTY OF A BED

I am wooden, pine, simple, straight and comfy,
What more can a bed be?
Loyal, I suppose,
I mean I am here when she leaves and here when she's home,
Well I guess I can't go anywhere.

She leaps out of bed, leaving my cosy, warm mattress,
Throwing my clean covers to the ground,
Complaining about the freezing cold.
What about me! I cry in vain, now I have no bed covers
And I won't see them till bedtime.

Slam! Gone! Nothing!
An eerie silence, an empty room.
Tick-tock, the clock winks at me
And the wardrobe smiles, slightly. Silence.
Minutes feel like hours, hours - years.

She's older now, taller, mature.
I am getting older too, worn out and cracking legs.
Bedtime's getting later, I'm not needed as much.
Maybe I'll be replaced soon, I just don't know.
I just don't know, anymore.

Sarah Hewson (13)
Tormead School

WARDROBE

Looking out into the world from my little corner of the room,
Feeling grand and powerful.
Each morning, I see a small girl arise from her bed,
Except she is not so small any more.
Her hair has grown and she is a lot taller,
She picks a different piece of clothing each day now,
Not as she used to, that smart green and white uniform,
And as she leaves each morning, precisely on time,
The room is left motionless
Except for the ticking of the clock in the far right-hand
                                    corner of the room
And the occasional creak of the door as the wind blows.
I look at the room now and examine it as I always do.
It is so neat, not a speck of dust anywhere.
It fills me with joy to know I am being useful to her,
Although I don't think that I am as useful now as I used to be.
Her clothes are bigger and take up more room,
Not like they used to when she was a little girl.
She looks at me each day now, I can tell it is a sad look.
It makes me sad too, I know what is coming,
She is going to leave and start a new life without me.

Jackie Lydon (14)
Tormead School

TIME

Sometimes there is too much,
Sometimes there is not enough.

When there is too much time
I do nothing
When there is too little
I do too much,
I don't know how to balance the two.

There is a blank page
and too much time,
I can't fill the page
and time takes its place.

But when I sing,
time flies
and time means nothing.

Charlotte Catchpole (11)
Wispers School

'JUST DO AS I SAID!'

'Just do as I said,' cried Mum to I,
As soon as I'd finished my tea,
'Just do as I said, and please go away,
Don't hang around bothering me.'

'Just do as I said,' cried Mum to I,
As soon as I'd finished my drink,
'Oh, please go away, stop bothering me,
Just leave me to sit down and think.'

'Just do as I said,' cried Mum to I,
As soon as I'd finished my bath,
'I'm starting to get cross, you know what to do,
Do you have to just stand there and laugh?'

'Just what did you say Mum,
And then I'll go to bed,
As soon as you've finished thinking,
Just what was it you said?'

Harriet Woolf (12)
Wispers School

MY LAST HALLOWE'EN

'Trick or treat, trick or treat' I scream and run around,
Laughing and chatting and rolling on the ground.
We knock on all the doors in town,
Waiting for our treat to hopefully be found.

I bang loudly on one big door.
Nothing happens, so I bang some more.
An old man suddenly appears from within
And says, 'Good heavens children, you're fit for the bin!'
We gave a gasp and asked for our treat,
He turned around and slammed the door,
And we could hear the patter of his feet.

We studied the words in our rhyme,
'Trick or treat,' we started to chime.
The man came back, his face all red,
How did we know we were going to be dead?
He asked us in and we agreed,
He gave us chocolate and he started to read.
The book he read was called 'The Curse of Hallowe'en.'

I started to shudder as my face went green,
I was nearly sick with the words he read:
'Sleep my children, got to bed for soon you all will be
                                                    lying dead!'
We all screamed and headed for the door,
Then, there was no more . . .

Olivia Johnson (12)
Wispers School

SAVE THE SPIDERS!

The spider has eight legs
And he begs and begs and begs
That you won't knock over his nest
Which has lots of tiny eggs
So please, don't be a pest.
The spider crawls around
But he daren't go out of bounds,
'Cause he is too scared if we come
To knock over his nest with our thumb,
So please, don't be a meanie
And make their population teenie.

Emily Webb (12)
Wispers School

THE BIG, BLACK DOG

The big, black dog that sits by the door,
Staring at me while licking his paws.
His soft leather pads on the bottom of his feet,
Felt soft on the hand, but rough on the feet,
His wet, rubber nose covered with black,
Was cold, but dry when the sun came back.
The big, black dog that sits by the door,
I'm wondering, wondering more and more
About the big, black dog that sits by the door.

Hannah Keywood (12)
Wispers School

THE STALKER

He's right behind you
You know he's there
You turn a corner
You turn with fear
His beady eyes are watching you
He makes no sound
You look around
He makes it look as if he's going his way
You turn around and move away
It's getting colder
You shrug a shoulder
You begin to jog
Breaking into a run
You think about where you are going
As you feel his presence behind you
You hear his feet
As your own heart beats
Faster and faster
You turn the handle as fast as you can
You slam the door
And collapse onto the floor
He rings the bell
Seconds after you fell
You peer through the cat flap
As he begins to tap
He shouts, 'Miss, Miss'
You open the door a fraction
He holds out a piece of paper
And says, 'You dropped this.'

Stacey McGillivray (12)
Wispers School

SCHOOL

School is fun like my games and drama lesson
With the really cool teacher, Mr Sheppard.
School can be both interesting and boring,
But it is good when you meet new friends.
School can be hard when you are doing exams
But spelling is not so bad!

Practising Mavis Beacon keeps me in touch
Whilst IT keeps my work neat.
In music there is lots of singing
And our French teacher counts un, deux, trois.
In Spanish, we ask 'Que hora es?'
But in History, we go back in time.

School is all of these rolled into one,
Come to Wispers and join our fun.

Cara Smith (11)
Wispers School

PUPPY POWER

I wish I was a little puppy again,
I would I could run around and play,
I wish I could go for nice long walks,
Without getting tired straight away,
I wish kids would pet me in the streets again,
I wish I was a little puppy again.

Amie Simpson (12)
Wispers School

RING THE BELLS

Ring the bells make them cry,
Run them down till they die.
Light the candles make a feast,
They'll rage if you call them beasts.

Race downstairs shut the doors,
Shut the windows make a pause,
Look outside hear the wind,
The face of a dolly is thoroughly pinned.

Forget your thoughts but don't cry,
When you tell the story, don't you dare lie,
But that's if you have a chance,
You heard a ghost and saw a glance.

Fiona Feuk (12)
Wispers School

HALLOWE'EN

It's Hallowe'en Night,
We sit waiting for their calls.
Ding-dong chimes the front door bell,
It's a good job I have a bowl of sweets
At my feet.
Witches, ghosts, wizards and a cat with a mouse
Off they go to another house.

Hannah Drummond (12)
Wispers School

HALLOWE'EN

It was Hallowe'en Night,
When the moon was bright as the mist swept tight.

Fears lingered down my body
For all of you were scared.

All spooky noises gave a trance, as I gave a prance
the pumpkins gave me a glance.

You could hear the wicked witches appear,
as I shed a tear and a stomach full of fear.

For it was only Hallowe'en.

Antonia Hall (13)
Wispers School

THE MOON

She shines brightly and her shadow figures behind her
She lights up the world with her brilliant radiance
The cloud's shape sometimes looks like a witch flying over the moon.
Every night she's there watching over everybody
She's so far away yet she feels so close,
You wonder if she will ever last.

Samantha Tidy (11)
Wispers School

A COLD AUTUMN'S DAY

As I walk outside on a cold autumn's day,
Through the leaves I make my way,
Horse chestnuts fall from the trees high,
Under the leaves the hedgehogs lie.

Cold wind blows the trees around,
The sycamores twirl to the ground
Dew in the grass where the fairies hide
The darker it gets I walk inside.

Katie Boyle (11)
Wispers School

THE OLD MAN

A towering giant,
His skin is like paper,
all wrinkly and dark.
Standing sternly,
heels dug in the ground.
When he breathes over me,
it's like snow dripping down my back,
sending a cold sensation, in my body.
His stern look, freezes me.

Rosanna Curran (11)
Wispers School

A Touch Of Autumn

Red, yellow, pink and green
All the colours you've ever seen.
The robin and thrush sing a proud melody
As the gardener plunges into the dampened ground
The acorns hang from the sky as pixie houses
Beautiful and shy.
The spider slays in his web
And the nettles protect his only bed.
Horse chestnuts a porcupine spine
To keep out unwanted visitors from his tender nut.

The lady of the wood will stand with elegance in her bower
Recreating every hour.
The dew will glisten in the light
And sparkles at the dawn of night.
Blackberries a birds feast all sweet and sour
A love to some and others not
The apples are an inner child
Bringing out the happiness meek and mild.
The old man's beard grey and soft
And the lamb's tail will never die
Opening next spring to the world
It will keep hope to a lonely child.
The seeds that float around are the flower fairies
That bless the ground and all living flowers and plants
So hail for autumn and its beauty divine.
Its one and only touch of frost
Its heart and song.
It's spirit will keep the glee
For everyone for you and me.

Arabella Field (11)
Wispers School

NIPO AND CALIPO

Once there was a hippo called Nipo
Who had a girlfriend called Calipo
They got married while on tour
The day before
Their friends all died of Manzipo.

The two loved ones were now all alone
Having to celebrate on their own
So they sailed down the river
And slept in a tiver
And drank all night on their own.

When the sun shone bright in the morning
Nipo and Calipo were yawning
Calipo was ill
So she took a pill
And they thought she would be better next morning.

Calipo wasn't better next morning
So they called out Doctor Cavornee
He was also a hippo
And his real name was Flippo
And he said she had caught the Manzipo.

They were very upset it was shocking
So they decided to go Sunday shopping
Nipo bought her a dress
For ninety-five pence
And when he got back she was dead.

Stephanie Hamilton (11)
Wispers School

APOLOGY

Dear Mrs What's-your-name,

I know you'll be busy moving in,
I just want to clear a few things up *before* we begin.
I'm sorry about the posters superglued to your door,
It was me who put them there (but I was only four).

Now the matter of what came through the windows -

I know there are lots of balls inside the house,
And somewhere a *large* pet mouse.
I would have relieved you of them all,
But you see the holes in the windows are for me a little small.

The matter of the rather hungry animals -

I'm sorry for the inconvenience of the rattler and boa constrictor,
But you really shouldn't blame me I brought then from Victor.
I must warn you about my mistake of the crocodile from the lake,
But by now you must realise your life *is* at stake.

As Johnny's mother I must add,
That indeed my son is very bad,
If you find an atomic bomb,
I do realise it is very wrong,
But it is his favourite toy,
And Johnny really is a harmless boy!

Fiona Joy Ismay (11)
Wispers School

MY DOG CALLED WHISKY

I have a dog called whisky
Who is terribly frisky.
He loves the sea
He bounds to me
My lovely dog called Whisky.

I have a dog called Whisky
Being with him is risky.
He eats my food
Acts like a dude
My cool dog called Whisky.

I have a dog called Whisky
Who is completely mucky
He runs for miles
He always smiles
My champion dog called Whisky.

I have a dog called Whisky
Who makes our lives so tricky
He digs holes in the lawn
Then eats cheese prawns
My naughty dog called Whisky.

Rebecca Jayne Booker (12) Wispers School &
Benjamin David Booker (9) Kings College Junior School